COACH'S GUIDE TO SUCCESS

Contents

Introduction

Everyday Woman Authors and Readers,

Welcome to Coach's Guide to Success—our 10th published book under the Everyday Woman brand. As we hold this milestone in our hands, we're filled with pride, gratitude, and awe at what happens when women come together to share their stories, their wisdom, and their purpose.

This book is more than just pages and chapters. It's a living, breathing example of what we believe at Everyday Woman—that when women rise, they lift others with them. With over 300 women featured across our book series so far, we are actively building what we call our 10,000 Women. 10,000 Voices. 10,000 Legacies. movement. And this book brings us one step closer.

Every woman in Coach's Guide to Success has poured her knowledge, passion, and real-life experience into her chapter to support, uplift, and empower others. These are coaches, leaders, and change-makers who are walking the walk, and we are honored to give them a platform to shine. Their stories don't just offer advice—they offer possibility, perspective, and power.

To the women featured in this book: thank you for trusting us to share your brilliance. To the readers holding this book: may you find the inspiration, tools, and reminders you need to move boldly toward your own definition of success. And to every woman still holding her story inside—your voice matters, and we can't wait to help you share it with the world.

Xoxo Galit & Angela
Co-Founders of Everyday Woman

CHAPTER ONE

By Galit Ventura-Rozen

Galit Ventura-Rozen

Everyday Woman

Co-Founder

Broker/Owner - Commercial Professionals,

CEO -Empowering U

www.galitventurarozen.com

www.linkedin.com/in/galitventurarozen

www.instagram.com/galitventurarozen

www.facebook.com/galit.rozen.9

Galit started her entrepreneurial career 28+ years ago in commercial real estate. She is Broker/Owner of Commercial Professionals and has sold over $700 million in properties. She is the Co-Founder of Everyday Woman. She is a paid professional speaker and has spoken all over Canada and the United States on leadership, effective communication, mindset, and more. She works with women privately to show them how to "Elevate their Brand" through methods that have worked for her and her businesses. She is the author of The Successful Woman's Mindset, her solo book, and ten books she has put together with over 300 female authors for Everyday Woman.

The Power of Accountability

By Galit Ventura-Rozen

Let's be honest—if building a successful business were easy, everyone would do it.

But you, you're not just anyone. You're a woman with a dream. You've started something. Maybe you've launched an online business, built a brand, or dipped your toes into coaching, consulting, or selling a product or service that lights your heart on fire. You know you're meant for more.

But let me ask you something, woman-to-woman:

How many times have you made a plan to finally go all in on your business… and then didn't follow through?

How many times have you set a goal, only to watch it quietly fade into the background of laundry, errands, work, and taking care of everyone else?

You're not lazy. You're not unmotivated. You're not incapable.

You're just missing one powerful thing: accountability.

And I get it—when you're the boss, there's no one watching over your shoulder. There's no one to tell you to get that newsletter written, record that video, launch that offer, or follow up with those leads. The freedom that drew you to entrepreneurship can quickly become the very thing that keeps you stuck.

So, how do we fix that?

Let's talk about the power of accountability—real accountability—and why it might be the missing piece between where you are and the success you're craving.

Why We Struggle to Hold Ourselves Accountable

If you're a woman, chances are you've spent most of your life putting others first.

You've been the caretaker, the peacemaker, the rock for everyone else. You've been dependable, loyal, responsible… and somewhere in all that giving, you started neglecting yourself.

Now you're trying to build a business—a dream—and you're realizing it's going to take a new version of you to get there. A version that stops breaking promises to herself. A version that sets a goal… and follows through.

But here's what I want you to hear loud and clear:

You don't have to do it alone.

In fact, you shouldn't.

Accountability Is Not Shame—It's Support

Let's clear something up. Accountability is not about guilt trips, pressure, or someone breathing down your neck. That's not empowerment—that's punishment.

True accountability is about having someone who believes in you and holds you to your highest standard.

It's about someone calling you forward, not calling you out.

It's about locking arms with someone who won't let you shrink, settle, or hide.

When you're building a business, especially online, where it's easy to isolate, it's easy to tell yourself things like:

"I'll do it tomorrow."

"No one's watching anyway."

"It's not that big of a deal if I skip this week."

But here's the truth: every time you don't follow through on what you said you would do, you chip away at your confidence.

And every time you do follow through, especially when it's hard, you build trust with yourself. That's what accountability helps you do—build that muscle of self-trust.

My Wake-Up Call with Accountability

Let me tell you a quick story.

When I started in the coaching business 9 years ago, I was running my business from the corner of my living room. I had goals, ideas, and notebooks full of plans… but I was stuck. I wasn't showing up the way I wanted to. I was overthinking, procrastinating, and saying things like, "I'll start Monday," more than I'd like to admit.

One day, I decided to hire a business coach. A woman, just like me, heart-led, ambitious, juggling life and business. We met twice a month. We set goals out loud. I reported back on whether or not I followed through.

Let me tell you—everything changed.

Suddenly, I was no longer willing to break promises to myself, because I wasn't just showing up for me anymore—I was showing up for my business coach. And that momentum was contagious.

I got braver.

I got bolder.

I got better.

And that's when I realized that accountability isn't a luxury for entrepreneurs—it's a necessity.

3 Types of Accountability Every Woman Needs

If you're serious about building your online business, here are three types of accountability you need in your life:

1. Self-Accountability (Yes, It Starts with You)

Before relying on anyone else, you have to take responsibility for your dreams. That means:

Write down your goals.

Setting deadlines.

Tracking your progress.

Be honest with yourself when you fall short, and celebrate yourself when you rise.

Pro tip: Get yourself a visual system. Whether it's a whiteboard, a planner, or a sticky note wall, don't keep your goals in your head. Make them visible and tangible.

2. People Accountability (Don't Do It Alone)

Get around women who are on a similar journey. This could be:

A business bestie you meet with weekly.

A Facebook group with real engagement.

A coach who challenges and supports you.

A mastermind or group program where you check in consistently.

These are the people who will remind you of your greatness when you forget. They'll help you course-correct, cheer you on, and hold the mirror up when you need to get back on track.

3. Public Accountability (Say It Out Loud)

There's something powerful about saying your goals out loud. Post it on social media. Share it with your email list. Tell your community what you're working on.

Why? Because once you declare it, it becomes real.

You'll show up differently when other people are watching—not because of pressure, but because of purpose.

Accountability + Action = Results

Let me break it down simply:

Accountability without action is just talking.

Action without accountability is inconsistent.

But when you put the two together? That's where the magic happens.

You get clarity. You build confidence. You see results.

You stop spinning in circles and start moving in alignment.

You stop hiding behind "someday" and start showing up like the CEO you are.

And let's be honest—when you start seeing results, when the sales start coming in, when your inbox lights up with "YES!" replies, you'll realize: you were never unqualified or incapable—you were just unaccountable.

How to Start Using Accountability Today

You don't need a fancy plan to start. Here's how to put this into action now:

Choose one business goal for the next 30 days.

Make it clear, measurable, and meaningful.

Tell someone you trust.

A coach, friend, or business group. Share the goal and the deadline.

Set weekly check-ins.

These can be simple: Did I do what I said I would do? What's next?

Celebrate progress, not just perfection.

Every step forward is worth recognizing. Don't wait until the finish line to feel proud.

You Are Not Meant to Do This Alone

If no one's told you this lately, let me be the one to say it:

You are not too late.

You are not too old.

You are not behind.

You are exactly where you need to be to take the next brave step.

You have the vision. You have the wisdom. You have the passion.

Now, bring in the accountability to activate it.

And if you're thinking, "I don't know anyone to hold me accountable,"—guess what?

You do now.

Let this chapter be your nudge. Let me be that voice in your ear, reminding you:

You can do this—but you don't have to do it alone.

It's time to stop hoping, waiting, or winging it.

It's time to rise, show up, and lead like the woman you were always meant to be.

Unfiltered. Unstoppable. And held accountable every step of the way.

When you start holding yourself accountable—not just once in a while, but consistently—everything begins to shift.

You stop waiting for the "perfect time" and realize this is the perfect time.

You stop looking around for permission and realize you already have the power.

You stop playing small, and you start walking boldly in your purpose.

You wake up with clarity instead of confusion.

You move with intention instead of impulse.

You make decisions based on your vision, not your fear.

And the best part?

You begin to experience the joy, freedom, and fulfillment that comes from monetizing your passion and purpose.

You realize that you're not just building a business—you're creating a life.

You're helping people. You're making an impact. You're using your voice, your story, and your skills to serve others and create real transformation—not only for them but for yourself and your family.

You're no longer just "trying something out." You're building something meaningful.

Yes, there will still be hard days. But now you have tools. You have support. And you have you—the version of you who shows up, even when it's tough.

That's what accountability unlocks.

It's not about hustle—it's about honoring your calling.

So here's your invitation: Be the woman who follows through. Be the woman who shows up for her dreams. Be the woman who doesn't just talk about success—she lives it.

Because when you mix passion with purpose, add consistency, sprinkle in some courage, and anchor it all in accountability, you become unstoppable.

And that is what success is made of.

CHAPTER TWO

Angela Giles
Giles Enterprises
CEO
Everyday Woman
Co-Founder

www.angelagiles.com
www.linkedin.com/in/angelakaygiles www.instagram.com/angelaksgiles www.facebook.com/AngelaKayGile

Angela Giles is a marketing pioneer and a passionate communicator and mentor who is driven to help her clients become successful and effective in their fields. With nearly 20 years of experience in business and digital marketing, she has an innate skill to connect with

audiences of diverse backgrounds. She has helped over 2,000 business owners generate over $ 50 million in sales during the past 20 years. Her goal for each training is that each audience member leaves inspired, confident, and ready to implement change.

Entrepreneurial Resilience: Thriving Through Challenges and Change

By Angela Giles

The year I lost everything didn't start with a crash.

There were no sirens. No dramatic hospital visits. No red flags waving wildly in front of me.

It started quietly—an ache I couldn't shake, an exhaustion I couldn't explain, a heaviness in my chest that lingered longer than it should have. Initially, I followed the typical path of most entrepreneurs.

I powered through it.

I told myself it was stress. I convinced myself it was just part of the hustle. I believed I could push through it like everything else life had thrown at me.

But bodies have a way of telling the truth when our minds won't listen.

Eventually, that quiet ache roared into something I couldn't ignore. My body shut down. And just like that, the business I had built, the schedule I had maintained, the life I had curated—stopped.

I had spent years building my business, showing up for clients, hosting events, launching programs, and driving forward at breakneck speed. But when your health fails, none of that matters. My body had been whispering, then nudging, and now screaming for me to pay attention.

The diagnosis was serious. Life-altering.

I won't go into every medical detail here, but what I will tell you is this: in that moment, I had a choice.

I could keep trying to run the same race—or I could surrender. And not surrender in a way that meant giving up, but surrender in a way that meant finally letting go of what no longer served me.

That's the moment everything began to change.

The Collapse Before the Rise

When your identity is wrapped up in achievement, success feels like oxygen.

So when you have to stop producing, stop performing, and start receiving—grace, support, healing—it's not just a physical reckoning. It's a spiritual one.

I wasn't just healing my body. I was unraveling the beliefs I had inherited about worth, productivity, and survival.

For the first time in years, I had to stop.

And in that stillness, I heard a new voice.

It didn't sound like the hustle. It didn't sound like urgency. It didn't sound like pressure.

It sounded like the truth.

It said, You don't have to earn rest. You don't have to prove your value. You get to build something new.

It was like standing at the edge of the ocean after a storm—the waves still rough, the sky still dark—but knowing deep in my soul that sunrise was coming. That there was more for me on the other side of this.

And there was.

But it didn't come all at once. Healing required more than time—it required trust.

Starting Over—By Design

Recovery was not linear. There were good days, hard days, and days that didn't feel like progress at all. But somewhere along the way, a fire began to build in me again.

This time, it wasn't about going back. It was about building forward—with intention, with alignment, and with a new way of doing life and business.

I realized I didn't want to return to the business model I had before. It was profitable, yes—but it wasn't sustainable. It didn't leave room for life. It didn't leave space for softness, creativity, or rest. It required me to be "on" 24/7—and I had barely survived it.

I had outgrown it.

So I did what entrepreneurs do best when they're aligned: I built something new.

I rebuilt my business from the ground up. I leaned into simplicity. I got radically clear on what I wanted my life to look like—and then I made the business serve that vision, not the other way around.

I let go of perfectionism. I stopped trying to be everywhere. I gave myself permission to make my business more human—and more powerful because of it.

I focused on high-impact, high-value offers that didn't depend on my constant presence.

I delegated with discernment.

I created systems that supported me when my energy was low.

And I told the truth—online and offline—about where I had been and what I had learned.

The way I showed up online changed. I wasn't interested in pretending anymore. I wasn't interested in curating a brand that looked perfect but felt hollow.

I wanted to be real and magnetic because of that realness.

Lessons in Resilient Entrepreneurship

What emerged wasn't just a new business—it was a new way of being in business.

And if you're reading this because you're in your own season of challenge, burnout, recovery, or reinvention, I want to share with you what I learned on the way back.

These aren't just tips. They're anchors. They're the principles that allowed me to not just survive, but thrive.

1. Burn It Down if You Need To

Sometimes, the most powerful thing you can do is walk away from what no longer serves you. Whether it's a toxic client, an outdated offer, or a business model that's killing your joy, let it go.

You're allowed to evolve.

Your business can grow with you—but only if you stop clinging to what worked in the past.

Let go of the old so you can create space for the new.

2. Build with Boundaries

One of the biggest shifts I made was deciding that rest was a business strategy.

I set work hours. I honored them. I stopped glorifying overwork. I made space in my calendar for living, not just launching.

Boundaries aren't about keeping people out; they're about setting clear expectations. They're about keeping you in alignment.

Actual growth doesn't come from more hours. It comes from deeper alignment.

3. Let the Right People In

Recovery taught me that you can't—and shouldn't—do it all alone. I hired help. I invested in mentorship. I leaned into the community.

You don't need to be the hero of every story.

Let people help you rise.

Asking for support isn't a weakness. It's wisdom.

4. Create Systems That Scale (Even When You Can't)

When my energy was low, my systems carried me. Automated marketing, repeatable client processes, pre-built funnels—these things weren't just time-savers. They were lifelines.

Resilience in business means preparing for the moments when you can't be 100%.

Smart systems create freedom and safety, and protect your progress when life interrupts your plans.

5. Build Something That Can Hold You

Your business should be strong enough to support you, not the other way around.

If your business only works when you're at full capacity, it's time to rethink the foundation.

Freedom comes when your business can function, grow, and serve without requiring you to be constantly available.

Your business should grow with you, not at the cost of you.

A New Kind of Success

Today, my business is thriving—not in spite of what I went through, but because of it.

I show up from overflow, not an obligation.

I speak from truth, not performance.

I lead with clarity, not chaos.

My health challenge broke me open—but it also rebuilt me with wisdom I never would have accessed otherwise.

I became more resilient. More honest. More intentional. And yes, more successful than I ever was before.

But this version of success feels different.

It feels sustainable. Soulful. Aligned.

And most importantly, it feels mine.

There's no chasing. No proving. Just becoming.

If You're In It Right Now…

Maybe you're reading this while you're in your version of the valley.

Maybe it's health. Or grief. Or burnout. Or just the quiet knowing that something in your business no longer fits.

Let me say this to you: You are not broken. You are being invited into something new.

Resilience isn't just about pushing through; it's about embracing the challenges that come with it. It's about learning to pause, pivot, and rise in a different way.

You don't have to go back to who you were. You're not supposed to.

You get to choose a new way.

Let this be your turning point.

Let this be your rebirth.

And know this—there is no timeline for transformation. Take all the time you need, but don't forget this one truth:

You are still becoming.

Final Words: Let This Be Your Invitation

You are allowed to do business differently.

You are allowed to rest.

You are allowed to evolve.

You are allowed to build a business that supports your whole life—not just your income goals.

The path of an entrepreneur is rarely a straight line. But in every bend, in every breakdown, there's the opportunity to return to something more profound:

Your truth.

Your vision.

Your voice.

Your power.

Let this be your reminder: Resilience isn't what keeps you going—it's what remakes you when everything changes.

And from that place?

You don't just rebuild.

You rise.

CHAPTER THREE

Anna Krolikowska
Anna K Law/ Anna P. Krolikowska PC
Attorney, Mediator, Collaborative Divorce Professional

www.annaklaw.com
Facebook.com/AttyKrolikowska
https://linktr.ee/annaklawchicago

Anna Krolikowska is a divorce attorney, mediator and a collaborative divorce practitioner working with clients in Chicago and its suburbs. Anna helps her clients have better divorce experiences and divorce outcomes. Her clients divorce with dignity and respect and preserve their co-parenting relationship. Anna believes that educating her clients about their legal and financial options empowers them to make better choices and build a better future for themselves and their families.

Anna is a Past President of the Illinois State Bar Association (ISBA) and only the 5th woman elected President of the ISBA since its inception in 1877. She has been recognized and honored for her work as a divorce attorney by her fellow attorneys and clients, and named one of the Best Lawyers in America by Best Lawyers- US News Report (2023, 2024, 2025), a Super Lawyer (2019-2025) and one of "Salute to Women Lawyers in Illinois" (2021), one of the "40 Under Forty" (2019), and a Leading Lawyer (2021-2024) by the Chicago Daily Law Bulletin as well as one of the Best 15 Lawyers in 2024 by MSN.

Anna currently serves as Chair of the Board of Directors of the ISBA Mutual Insurance Company, and is only the 4th woman elected chair of the board. Anna has also been elected and currently serves as the IL State Delegate to the American Bar Association (2023–2026), a member of the Executive Council of the National Conference of Bar Presidents (NCBP) (2022-2025), and one of the twelve appointed Commissioners of the ABA Commission on Women in the Profession.

Anna is a a former law school professor, a best selling author ("Everyday Woman's Guide to Thrive in Your Busy Life", "Iconic Woman's Guide to Empowerment"), and a frequent lecturer and speaker on issues related to divorce, leadership, women in business, networking and rainmaking, women in the legal profession, corporate governance, strategic planning, and life and work balance.

Anna is the author of a unique illustrated children's book series, which she wrote to help parents discuss divorce with their children and help families create brighter futures as they navigate through divorce, of which “"My Parents Are Getting Divorced"” and “"Emma's New Holidays"” have been published. Additional books about Emma and her parents will be published later in 2025. For more information on Emma and “My Parents Are Getting Divorced”, please visit www.myparentsaregettingdivorced.com or purchase the first installment of Emma's Journey Book 1: My Parents Are Getting Divorced (The Family We Will Be – A Heartfelt Children's Book Series About Navigating Divorce Together) https://a.co/d/9K9MpG1

To learn more about your divorce options or discuss speaking opportunities with Anna, contact her at anna@annaklaw.com or (847) 715-9328.

Follow Anna on Facebook.com/AttyKrolikowska, on Instagram:@Annaklawchicago, on LinkedIn https://www.linkedin.com/company/annaklaw, or Twitter @AKrolikowska5

The Power of Purpose: Achieving Success with Grace, Grit, and Balance

By Anna Krolikowska

When I started my career, I thought success was a straight line: set a goal, work hard, and voilà—dream achieved. Reality, as you probably know, looks more like a squiggly line with a few dead ends, wrong turns, and a whole lot of detours. But here's the thing about that winding path: it's where the magic happens. It's where we grow, learn, and develop the grit that makes us unstoppable.

As a business owner, professional leader, both corporate and nonprofit board director, wife, and a busy mom, I've learned a thing or two about thriving in chaos and staying focused on what really matters. My journey hasn't been perfect, and I'm glad—it's the messy parts that have taught me the most. Whether you're building a business, climbing the corporate ladder, or balancing both, here are some insights I hope will inspire you to move forward with courage, purpose, and clarity and build a life you love.

Define Your "Why"—And Let It Be Your Compass

Every great endeavor starts with a clear "why." What drives you to wake up in the morning and chase your goals? Is it your family? Your passion for helping others? A desire to create something bigger than yourself?

Your "why" is more than a motivational poster. It's the foundation of everything you do. When the road gets tough—and it will—your "why" will keep you grounded. It will remind you why you're putting in the effort, making the sacrifices, and stepping out of your comfort zone.

For me, my "why" is simple: I want to build a life where my professional success empowers my family, not detracts from it. I want my kids to see that hard work and kindness can coexist and that it's possible to lead with both strength and grace. Knowing my "why" helps me prioritize, say no to distractions, and stay focused on the bigger picture.

Take some time to reflect on your own "why." Write it down. Keep it visible. Let it guide your decisions. When you're clear on your purpose, you'll find the courage to take risks, the resilience to bounce back from setbacks, and the discipline to stay the course.

Embrace Progress, Not Perfection

If you're anything like me, you've had moments where you've set impossibly high standards for yourself. We want to excel in our careers, be perfect parents, stay on top of every committee, and still find time for ourselves. Spoiler alert: it's not possible—not all at once.

The sooner we embrace progress over perfection, the sooner we can start making real strides. It's not about getting everything right every single time; it's about showing up, learning, and improving as we go.

One of the best lessons I've learned is the power of delegation. Early in my career, I was convinced that doing everything myself was the only way to ensure success. Now, I know better. Whether it's hiring the right team members, outsourcing tasks, or simply asking for help, delegation frees you up to focus on the things that truly move the needle.

Remember: done is better than perfect. Give yourself permission to let go of the little things and focus on what matters most.

Build a Network That Lifts You Up

Success isn't a solo journey—it's a team sport. No one achieves greatness without support, and the relationships you cultivate along the way can make all the difference.

Start by building a network of mentors, peers, and supporters who understand you and your vision, and want to see you succeed. These are the people who will cheer you on, give you honest feedback, and offer guidance when you need it most.

I've found some of my greatest breakthroughs have come from conversations with other women who understand the unique challenges of balancing ambition with everyday life. Whether it's through professional organizations, mastermind groups, or one-on-one relationships, connecting with others who share your values and goals can inspire you to dream bigger and take bolder steps.

And don't forget to pay it forward. Be the mentor you wish you had. Share your experiences, encourage others, and celebrate their successes. When women support each other, incredible things happen.

The Balancing Act: Prioritize What Matters

Let's talk about balance—the holy grail of every entrepreneur and working mom. I'll let you in on a secret: it's less about splitting your time evenly and more about being intentional with where you spend your energy.

Start by identifying your top priorities. What matters most in your personal and professional life? For me, my health, my family, and my business. Everything else gets filtered through that lens. If an opportunity or commitment doesn't align with my priorities, I don't hesitate to say no. But I want you to know that it took time and practice to get comfortable with saying no.

Balance also means recognizing that life has seasons. There are times when work takes center stage and other times when family needs more attention. The key is to be present in whatever season you're in and give yourself grace when things feel out of sync.

Fail Forward

Here's the thing about failure: it's inevitable. But it's also a phenomenal teacher. Every setback, misstep, and unexpected detour holds a lesson if you're willing to look for it.

In my own journey, some of my biggest failures have paved the way for my greatest successes. A botched presentation taught me the importance of preparation. A failed project rollout showed me the value of not pushing a deadline at all costs. These lessons didn't come easily, but they shaped me into the leader I am today.

Don't fear failure—embrace it. Take risks, try new things, and know that every stumble brings you one step closer to your goals. As the saying goes, "You either win, or you learn."

Take Care of the CEO—That's You

As women, we're often so busy taking care of everyone else that we forget to take care of ourselves. But here's the truth: you can't pour from an empty cup. If you want to succeed in the long term, self-care isn't optional—it's essential.

For me, self-care looks like setting boundaries around my time, getting enough sleep (most of the time), and carving out moments of quiet to recharge. It also means making time for the things that bring me joy, whether it's reading a good book, taking that workout class I like, taking a walk, or simply enjoying a cup of coffee in peace. It also means spending plenty of time with my little one playing, going to the park or the pool, or working on crafts. It's all about experiencing joy and happiness and enjoying life.

Think of self-care as an investment in your future success. When you're rested, re-charged, and energized, you're better equipped to tackle challenges and show up as your best self.

Celebrate the Wins—Big and Small

Finally, don't forget to celebrate your victories along the way. Success isn't just about reaching the finish line; it's about enjoying the journey.

Take time to acknowledge your progress, no matter how small it may seem. Did you land a new client? Take your team out for lunch. Finally, finish that daunting project? Treat yourself to something special. Even the act of pausing to reflect on your achievements can be incredibly empowering.

Celebrating your wins reminds you of how far you've come and motivates you to keep pushing forward. Plus, it's a great excuse to pop some champagne or buy that pretty scarf you've been eyeing.

Dream Big

Success isn't about being the smartest person in the room or having all the answers. It's about showing up with courage, staying true to your purpose, not giving up, and learning from every step of the journey.

As women entrepreneurs and leaders, we have the power to make an incredible impact, not just in our businesses but in the lives of those around us. So, embrace your unique gifts, trust your instincts, and don't be afraid to dream big.

Your path won't look like anyone else's, and that's the beauty of it. Keep moving forward, stay rooted in your "why," and remember that you are capable of achieving greatness.

Now, go out there and change the world—you've got this.

CHAPTER FOUR

Jennifer Kiser

JK Mastercoaching, Chroma "Confidence is Beautiful"

Master of Health Science, Alternative Medicine Clinician, Physiologist, Kinesiologist, Nutrition Specialist, Performance Coach, Rehabilitator, Master Certified Life Coach, Speaker, Author, Beauty Brand Owner

https://www.chromahairbeauty.com/

https://www.jkmastercoaching.com/book-online

www.linkedin.com/in/jennifer-kiser-816992230

www.instagram.com/jkmastercoaching

My name is Jennifer Kiser, and I have a passion for movement, nutrition, fitness, and wellness, and have been led to guide family, friends, and community since adolescence. I am a Master of Health Science (Logan Chiropractic University), alternative medicine clinician, physiologist, kinesiologist, nutrition coach, performance coach, mindset coach, program coordinator/writer, master life coach, author, and educational-motivational speaker with focus on identity, trauma, self-esteem, body image, and confidence (specifically to empower women). I am a bodybuilder, bikini division competitor, model, and coach. I have created, designed, and launched a beauty brand in 2024, Chroma "Confidence is Beautiful".

I have a passion to empower women and truly believe that all women have the capacity to be empowered! From my perspective, women empowering women creates a collaboration of support, strength, peace, trust, confidence, and healing. I look forward to leading, learning, and collaborating with knowledgeable, strong-minded, strong-willed, resilient, emotionally balanced, confident women. I vow to stand in the gap for the women who are reaching out for support, and I am thankful for those who have and continue to fill in the gap for me.

Empowered Women Dream, Learn, Transform, Create, Re-create, and impact together~

The Eye of the Storm

By Jennifer Kiser

Personal storms may quickly shift like the speed of lightning, devastating the landscape of our hearts and minds. "*Eye of the Storm*" is the moment of calm or peace in the middle of a chaotic or turbulent situation, much like the center of a hurricane. The "Eye of the Storm" represents finding serenity amidst significant challenges or stress, whereas "peace" represents that state of tranquility within the storm and clinging to faith in the midst of chaos. How does one create peace in the midst of the storm(s) of life, which often strike us abruptly and unexpectedly? Seasons of life are greatly aligned with the physical seasons of Earth. Seasons are a natural phenomenon caused by the Earth's axial tilt and orbit around the sun. Each season has its own distinct and unique characteristics and weather patterns. Life seems to flow fluently when we are in the season in which we are blessed with favor and abundance, but what happens when an abrupt shift of tragedy or catastrophe occurs? Physiologically speaking, the stress response is triggered by the release of hormones. Our mind and body will immediately respond to catastrophic events.

According to the *American Psychological Association (APA)'s* Stress in America survey results, stress is a common issue that affects millions of people every day.

Prevalence of Stress in the U.S.

37% of U.S. adults report feeling debilitated when they are stressed. 56% of employed U.S. adults report job stability as the most influential factor in causing stress. Around 27% of U.S. adults report feeling so stressed it causes an inability to function on most days. Violence and crime are a significant source of stress for 75% of U.S. adults. Younger U.S. women are more likely to report feeling overwhelmed by stress than older women, with 62% of women ages 18 to 34 reporting feeling entirely overwhelmed by stress the majority of the time, compared to 48% of women ages 35 to 44, 27% of women 45 to 64 and 9% of women 65 years and older.

The stress response can be triggered in an instant of time, yet calming that response varies according to the 'stress' or 'trauma' experienced and your ability to become internally calm to return to a "natural state", homeostasis.

Experiencing catastrophic events repeatedly for extended periods of time, such as abuse, abandonment, chronic illness, accidents and injuries, rape, financial instability, political warfare, and caring for a loved one who is chronically ill creates an extended or more intense physiological *stress response*, also known as "*trauma*". *Trauma* is your body's response to an intensely stressful event(s) or situation(s) that overwhelms one's psychological being. Living in a prolonged state of stress (or trauma) and high alert may be detrimental to your physical and mental health. Understanding and recognizing the prevalence and potential physiological effects of stress are crucial steps toward managing it effectively.

The unpredictability of tragic events can be particularly distressing and may extensively trigger a range of reactions that affect our mental and physical physiology, as well as behavior. Some of the *physical symptoms* that may appear include:

- Loss of energy or fatigue
- Headaches
- Nausea or vomiting

- Tightness in the chest
- Rapid heart rate
- Grinding of teeth
- Dry mouth or thirst
- Feeling shaky or weak
- Severe sweating
- Stomach pain or digestive problems

Tragedy can also trigger a wide range of *emotions* and changes in *mental well-being*. These may include:

- Intense anxiety
- Sadness or anger
- Feeling numb, hopeless, or powerless
- Excessive worry or unexplained guilt
- Feeling agitated or unable to relax
- Moodiness or irritability
- Trouble concentrating
- Ruminating or having flashbacks of the tragic event

Behavioral changes can also occur among those who have experienced traumatic events, including:

- Nightmares or disrupted sleep
- Becoming socially isolated

- Frequent crying or outbursts
- Changes in appetite or eating patterns
- Avoidance of certain places or people that resurface difficult memories or negative reactions
- Heavy smoking, drinking, or drug use

Disturbing events activate a structure in the brain responsible for detecting threats called the amygdala. It responds by sending out a shock to multiple body systems to prepare for defense. The sympathetic nervous system initiates action, stimulating the release of stress hormones, adrenaline, and noradrenaline that equip the body for a fight-flight-or-freeze response. Short-term fear, anxiety, shock, and anger/aggression are all normal responses to distress and trauma. Negative feelings dissipate as the crisis abates and the experience fades from memory, but in some instances, the distressing feelings may linger, interfering with day-to-day life. Living in defense mode and ever-vigilant to the possibility of threat, one may experience continued issues with physical pain or sleep, encounter turbulence in their professional and personal relationships, and begin to feel a diminishing sense of self-worth. Proactive, positive psychological changes after trauma are also possible when one acknowledges their challenges and views themselves as *survivors* rather than *victims* of unfortunate events or experiences. These can include *building resilience*, developing effective coping skills, and developing a *sense of self-efficacy*. Some people may undergo post-traumatic development and growth, forging stronger relationships, redefining their relationships with spiritual purpose or renewed meaning, and gaining an enhanced appreciation for life. Although it may sound contradictory, post-traumatic growth can exist right alongside PTSD. Two of the most important elements fostering *recovery* are the provision of *social support* and the establishment of a sense of *safety*. In addition, *lifestyle factors* such as eating healthy, exercising, avoiding alcohol and drugs, acquiring enough sleep, interacting with loved ones regularly, and engaging in self-care may aid with the relief of trauma symptoms and *promote recovery.* Discussing the event(s), especially sharing feelings with others who underwent similar experiences, may also be advantageous.

One may ask, "*What is resilience?*" and is it possible for "me" to build resilience? The answer is YES! *Resilience* is the process and outcome of successfully adapting to burdensome, threatening, or challenging life experiences, especially through mental, emotional, and behavioral flexibility and adjustment to internal and external demands. Factors contributing to how well people adapt to adversities are varied, including the perspective in which individuals view and engage with the world, the quality and availability of social resources, and definitive coping strategies. Psychological research demonstrates that the resources and skills associated with resilience can be proven to be cultivated and practiced.

Resilience is built through finding "*peace*" while in the midst of the storm. Finding tranquility, harmony, and serenity in the midst of the storm is possible through intentional, focused engagement of positive intervention on your behalf.

Spiritual peace is often described as an elusive, beautiful state that sometimes feels like searching for hidden treasure. Manifesting or achieving spiritual peace is a personal journey that can be cultivated through practicing meditation, mindfulness, prayer, or quietly spending time in nature. It involves nurturing and exploring your spiritual beliefs and discovering what resonates with you most. It's about discovering and maintaining a state of inner harmony amidst life's chaos. Finding an inner calm, balance, connection with your higher power, contentment, and mindfulness aids in manifesting spiritual peace.

Cognitive peace refers to a state of mental clarity and tranquility in your *thought* processes. Cognitive peace is a condition where your mind is free from overload, confusion, and conflict, allowing clear and effective thinking. Clear thinking, sustained focus, ability to organize thoughts systematically, mental freedom, freedom from cognitive biases, and effective problem solving are examples to help you understand that you are experiencing *cognitive peace*. Cultivating cognitive peace can involve practices like mindfulness, cognitive-behavioral techniques, regular mental breaks, and engaging in activities that stimulate the brain positively, like puzzles or learning new skills.

Emotional peace is characterized by a state of internal harmony, balance, contentment, and emotional stability. Inner peace is the *feeling* you have when you're entirely at ease with yourself and your surroundings, free from worries and anxieties that often invade your mind. Neuroscience demonstrates that experiencing peace activates specific regions of the brain associated with positive emotions and well-being. The prefrontal cortex, which plays a vital role in emotional regulation, lights up like a Christmas tree when people report feeling emotional peace. You may begin to feel *emotional peace* by practicing emotional balance, self-awareness, acceptance of emotions, resilience of setbacks, empathy, and compassion. *Emotional peace* may also be nurtured through practicing mindfulness, self-care, journaling, and seeking support from loved ones. It's important to create a space where you can process and express your emotions in a healthy and constructive manner.

It is undeniable that "*peace*" has a powerful impact on our physical and mental health and well-being. Experiencing *peace* may lead to a number of *physical health* benefits. Living in a state of peace can lower your blood pressure, reduce stress hormones like cortisol, and even boost immune function. *Peace* is a soothing balm for our overworked bodies, inducing opportunities for our bodies to rest and repair. *Peace* also cultivates our *mental health*, reducing symptoms of anxiety and depression, improving cognitive function, and enhancing overall life satisfaction. Nurturing inner *peace* explores these benefits in greater depth, offering insights into how we can cultivate peace for better emotional health. Personal storms may quickly shift like the speed of lightning, devastating the landscape of our hearts and minds, but finding your "Eye of the Storm," your inner peace, will create a stronghold in the midst of chaos.

"I have said these things to you, that in me you may have peace. In the world, you will have tribulation. But take heart; I have overcome the world." John 16:33.

I AM~

CHAPTER FIVE

Julie Gardiner
Talent Unleashed
Fractional AI Officer and Coach

Email: julie@talent-unleashed.com
www.talent-unleashed.com
www.linkedin.com/in/juliegardineruk/

Julie Gardiner is a trailblazing AI strategist and Fractional AI officer and Coach with over 35 years of experience in IT, finance, and telecommunications. As the founder of Talent Unleashed, Julie partners with organizations to craft and implement transformative AI strategies that drive innovation, optimize operations, and create measurable business impact. Leveraging her deep expertise, Julie helps businesses navigate the complexities of AI adoption, integrating cutting-edge solutions that align with strategic goals. As a fractional AI officer, she provides hands-on leadership in designing scalable AI initiatives, enhancing decision-making processes, and uncovering data-driven opportunities for growth.

Julie's innovative approach combines a practical understanding of AI's potential with a focus on ethical implementation, ensuring technology enhances, rather than disrupts, organizational values. Through Talent Unleashed, Julie empowers companies to harness AI as a competitive advantage, guiding them to achieve agility, efficiency, and long-term success in an increasingly AI-driven world.

AI: The Jetpack Every Coach Needs for Success

By Julie Gardiner

As a world-class coach and AI strategist, I've spent years honing my craft and finding innovative ways to deliver maximum value to my clients. Like many of you, I've been on a mission to not just meet expectations but exceed them. That's why I see Artificial Intelligence (AI) not as a tool to replace us but as a jetpack to propel our coaching practices to new heights. In this chapter, I'll share how AI can help us amplify our impact, streamline our processes, and unlock levels of scalability and efficiency we never thought possible.

Why AI is a Game-Changer for Coaches

AI isn't here to diminish the human touch—the heart of what makes coaching so powerful. Instead, it's here to empower us. Imagine AI as your silent partner, handling repetitive tasks, offering insights that might otherwise go unnoticed, and providing you with the time and mental clarity to focus on transformational work with your clients.

Setting You Up for Success

1. **From the Start** - Every great coaching journey begins with clarity, and AI is a master at helping you get there. Using tools like ChatGPT, you can create powerful prompts to guide you through the early stages of building your practice. Whether it's defining your niche, crafting your positioning statement, or developing your marketing strategy, think of these tools as

your own personal coach, helping you lay the foundation for a thriving business.

2. **Personalization at Scale** - One of the greatest challenges we face as coaches is balancing the need for deep personalization with the desire to reach more people. By analyzing session notes, feedback, and assessments, AI tools can uncover patterns, identify growth areas, and suggest tailored strategies for each client. With the right pre-prepared prompts, you can even use AI during sessions to assist with active listening, reframing, or generating curiosity-driven questions. It's like having a co-pilot who's always ready to support you.

3. **Reclaiming Your Time** - Let's be honest: administrative tasks are boring. Scheduling, tracking progress, and onboarding—these tasks are important but often detract from the time we could spend with clients or developing our skills. AI tools can automate these tasks, giving you hours back in your week to focus on what truly matters: coaching and growing your practice.

4. **Data-Driven Coaching Intuition** is a vital skill for any coach, but when paired with data-driven insights, it becomes unstoppable. AI tools can analyze vast amounts of client data to provide actionable insights, helping you make more informed decisions. Whether it's tracking progress, identifying blind spots, or evaluating the effectiveness of your strategies, data-backed coaching elevates the impact you can have on your clients' lives.

5. **Scaling Without Compromising Quality.** For many of us, the idea of scaling our practices feels daunting. How do you maintain the quality and depth of your coaching while expanding your reach? AI provides the answer. With tools like automated workflows, virtual assistants, and interactive platforms, you can engage with more clients without losing the personal connection

that sets your practice apart. AI makes it possible to grow without stretching yourself too thin.

Tools to Make AI Work for You

- There are countless AI-powered tools available (please reach out for the latest list), but here are some categories and examples to get you started:

1. Client Management and Scheduling: Keeping track of client details and managing appointments becomes effortless with tools like:

- Calendly: Automates scheduling and eliminates back-and-forth emails.
- HubSpot CRM: Organizes client information, communication history, and session notes.
- Acuity Scheduling: Manages appointment reminders, intake forms, and payments.

You could also create a chat bot to speak to your customers and book meetings for you and answer any queries about how you can work together.

2. Platforms for Delivering Coaching Streamline your service delivery with tools like:

- CoachAccountable: Combines session management, goal tracking, and progress reports.
- Kajabi: This lets you create and sell courses or manage memberships.

Create your own AI clone to help your clients outside of coaching sessions.

- LearnDash: Adapt learning paths based on your client's progress.

3. Virtual Assistants, LLM, and Chatbots: These tools can handle FAQs, engage clients, and support content creation.

   - ChatGPT: Assists with brainstorming, drafting content, and responding to queries.

   - Drift: Captures leads and engages website visitors in real-time.

4. Assessment and Feedback Tools: Evaluate and track client progress effectively with:

   - Gallup CliftonStrengths: Analyzes client strengths and offers tailored insights.

   - Coachmetrix: Tracks pre- and post-session surveys for measurable results.

   - Mentimeter: Collects real-time feedback during workshops or sessions.

5. Marketing and Content Creation: Stand out and attract clients with AI-powered marketing tools:

   - Jasper AI: Writes blog posts, emails, and social media content in your voice.

   - Canva: Suggests AI-powered design templates for stunning visuals.

6. Session Notes and Insights Capture every detail with tools like:

   - Otter.ai: Transcribes and summarizes coaching sessions.

- Revv: Analyzes recorded sessions for patterns and opportunities.
- Cogito: Provides real-time feedback on client engagement.

How ChatGPT Can Enhance Your Coaching

AI tools like ChatGPT are more than just helpful—they're game-changing. Here's how I use them in my practice:

- Summarizing Session Notes - After each session, I upload my notes or recordings, and ChatGPT helps by highlighting key themes and progress, identifying areas for future focus, and spotting recurring challenges or concerns.
- Generating Follow-Up Questions - ChatGPT excels at crafting thoughtful, open-ended questions that deepen reflection. For example: "I have session notes from previous coaching sessions with a client. The client has been working on [insert specific goal or challenge, e.g., improving communication skills or managing stress]. Based on this focus, suggest 5-10 open-ended questions I can use in our next session to help them reflect, gain deeper insights, and identify actionable steps. The questions should be tailored to the themes and progress from their past sessions."
- Preparing for Sessions - By reviewing past notes, ChatGPT helps me plan effectively. For instance: "Your client wanted to work on delegation. Consider asking, 'How did your new approach to delegation go this week?' or 'Did you notice any changes in team dynamics?'"
- Providing Resources and Exercises - ChatGPT offers ideas for books, journaling prompts, and exercises. For example: "I have a client who is struggling with imposter syndrome. Can you suggest A list of books that address imposter syndrome and

building self-confidence? Journaling prompts to help them reflect on and overcome feelings of self-doubt. Practical exercises they can try to reframe their negative self-talk and build their self-worth."

- Real-Time Feedback During Sessions - Even in live sessions, ChatGPT provides insights. A prompt like this helps me reframe client concerns:

"You are a world-class coach and are great at reframing concerns into opportunities. Take the following concern or fear, and give me three different reframes that can help shift the concern or fear and turn it into an opportunity or a new way of viewing the situation. You can decode the underlying belief or beliefs that sustain the concern or fear and speak to that to help loosen the concern or fear. Here is the statement or language that my client used that I want you to deliver to me a reframe for: {{Write your client's excuse or concern here}}. Now, take that and give me three different reframes. Give me a reframe on different levels and depths. The first one is on a surface level, the 2nd one is a reframing of the concerns or fears, and the 3rd one focuses on the beliefs that support that and reframes those into an opportunity and possibility. Also, choose a rich and vibrant metaphor that I can use in each of the reframes to deliver the reframe in an interesting metaphor format. Also, give me one additional reframe that is straightforward and simple to understand about how to redesign their perspective of concern or fear and have them see a new opportunity to feel willing to have more choices and move forward in light of their concern or fear."

Next Steps

Working with an AI Strategist can help you get started with putting on your jetpack and can be as simple as creating prompts for you, but if you'd prefer to do it for yourself, here are some tips for getting started

1. Start Small. Begin with one or two tools that address your immediate needs, and expand as you grow comfortable.
2. Learn the Tools. Invest time in understanding your chosen tools. Tutorials and support are your best friends.
3. Stay Human AI enhances, but it doesn't replace it. Maintain the personal touch that defines great coaching.
4. Keep Up with Trends: AI evolves quickly. Stay informed to keep your practice ahead of the curve.
5. Be Transparent. Share how AI supports your work with clients. Transparency builds trust and demonstrates your commitment to their success.

A Success Story: Sarah's AI Transformation

Sarah, a leadership coach, faced the challenge of scaling her practice. By leveraging tools like CoachAccountable for session management, Jasper AI for content creation, Otter.ai for transcription, and ChatGPT and Prompts, she scaled from 10 to 30 clients a month without sacrificing quality. Her jetpack? AI.

Final Thoughts

AI isn't just a tool; it's a jetpack for coaches. It's here to elevate what we do best, giving us the freedom, insights, and scalability to transform more lives. So strap in, explore the possibilities, and let AI propel your coaching practice to extraordinary heights.

CHAPTER SIX

Tracy Nosal
The Renegade Mentor

https://www.facebook.com/tracy.nosal
https://www.instagram.com/renegade_mentor/

The field of coaching is blooming in this new age of advisory. While each coach is unique, Tracy Nosal is in a field all her own. Having earned wisdom through depth of personal and professional experience, Tracy is uniquely equipped with the strength and grit essential to guide others to greater fulfillment.

Widely known as The Renegade Mentor, Tracy is sought after for her intuitive, no-nonsense way of awakening clients from the trances keeping them stuck. Teaching clients to grow into life's lessons as they unfold is central to Tracy's transformative approach. Though curriculums will vary, all journeys start similarly upon recognizing that our most raw moments of reckoning are, in actuality, fated invitations to rise to meet our higher selves.

Tracy answered her call and has since been deeply driven to deliver on her soul's purpose ,which ultimately led to a bold pivot from a successful business career. Today, Tracy focuses her fierce ambition towards fulfilling her life's work: guiding high-achieving warrior women to reclaim their power and realize their fullest potential.

Unlock Your Dynamic Power!

By Tracy Nosal

Unlocking your dynamic power takes balance in every area of your life. Have you ever stopped to acknowledge what it is that is out of balance in your life? These are the things that keep you from being fully attentive to thoughts and frequencies that affect personal power. Now, I'm not trying to say you should pretend like everything is perfect. You'd be fooling yourself. But, it is important for you to know that your thoughts and emotions have a frequency that affects everything you do and attract. If you are feeling focused on business but your personal relationships are in turmoil, then you are not your magnetic and powerful self. It's okay to admit that you are not where you want to be. You know that having it all together is a feeling. You do not have to put on a facade, and what a relief that is!

Unlocking your balanced yet dynamic self is to give yourself grace when something isn't quite right in your life. Being authentic allows for personal and professional growth. Accepting that you are a work in progress.

Take Time and Evaluate

While you take time to evaluate how things are in your life that are out of balance, that's when you can begin to shift. When part of your life is off, it drains your energy. The sense of not having things together will always be in the back of your mind, which will keep you from being dynamic overall. Accepting that there is emotional cleanup work to be done is the first step to transformation. You can not skip this part of your journey. Being dynamic means owning all of you and all the emotions that you feel. Healing old emotional pains and traumas will set you free.

Showing Up In Your Power

Are you a people pleaser? If so, you are giving away your power. You must show up for yourself first! I'm referring to how you feel as you go about your day. Yes, I understand you have responsibilities to attend to, like family and work. And I'm sure you are thinking about your to-do list and every which way you are being pulled. But if this leaves you feeling drained, then you are not standing in your power and allowing yourself to reach your full potential.

Starting your day quietly with a nice cup of coffee or tea as you ponder your day ahead will give way to a dynamic yet positive day. You will begin to notice how accomplished you feel with each task you complete.

Handling Stress

This is actually easier than you think because it's all in your mind. What I mean by that specifically is how you mentally and emotionally respond to stress. We all have it, but learning how to go neutral will keep your energy from spiraling downwards. And as we know, sometimes it can be hard to recover from the after-effects of stress. However, being in your power and having a solid headspace is how you can keep stress responses to a minimum. I know this can be a challenge. So, let's face it: there are just some things in life that really test us. If you face everything as it comes and work through your emotions, then you are becoming stronger in your essence and how you show up for life. The trick is to be calm and patient but powerful when a situation turns on a stress trigger. Your body will feel it and respond accordingly, which throws off a frequency that others in your space can feel. Take time to pause and think about what your response will cause before reacting to any given situation.

Unlock Your Dynamic Power

When you master your thoughts and emotions, you are in control of your energetic state of being. This will, in fact, take inner journey work, but this is where your treasures are found. The more you face those thoughts of "I'm not good enough" or "How can I possibly handle this task in front of me," the more you will begin to notice what the original experience was that created this thought pattern. I know most aren't connecting early childhood experiences to the present, but it is the very thing that is affecting your energy. As you grow and shift through life, your mental state becomes clearer if you put in the work to make it that way. Thus allowing you to be more vibrant. In an instance where negative thoughts arise, you will catch them and can then acknowledge why and what you need to shift.

Proverbial Glass Wall

Most people have white-knuckled their way to success. Head down and focused, but not realizing that at some point you will hit the proverbial glass wall. You know that point in life when you come up for air and realize that life is a mess and you are barely holding everything together? Some hit this point due to chronic stress that created a health issue, or their finances have been impacted. Whatever it is for you, this is the point of awareness that something needs to change. You need to change!

Shifting Awareness

When you are fully aware of how you handle life, you, in a sense, take a bird eye view of how you navigate your day-to-day tasks. This gives you a moment to view everything from a relaxed perspective, which allows you to be in control of how you navigate your journey. As you rise in awareness, you will recognize old thought patterns quicker than usual. And will allow you to take the wisdom while being able to release the old thoughts. You get to master your energy and what you choose to create in your life.

Mastering Energetics

The more you observe that your thoughts create how you experience life, the more you will want to master your personal energy. How you feel is how you energetically show up. This is where you begin to create positive outcomes in your life, as if by magic. You are energy! Of course, your thoughts are energy, too! Once you start mastering your energetics, you will start to have fun as you are the creator of how your life unfolds. Understanding it is about yourself and how you feel will greatly help you when bigger issues show up that can throw you off balance. The calmer you are, the more control you have over your life.

Balancing Emotions

The quicker you balance your emotions, the more at ease you will be, giving you clarity on what you are feeling and why. This is how you can have focused intentions. There will, of course, be situations that can cause extreme emotions, but this is your opportunity to take control and process what you are feeling. Staying calm and neutral allows you to stay in authority over your life. You will begin to notice how people respond to you. The more aware you become of how your body feels when your emotions are all over the place, the more you can break patterns and take control of your physical health.

Being Aligned

Now that you understand how your thoughts and emotions affect your life, you can grow to be in alignment. What does that mean? In order to utilize your energy, you must be aligned in peace and clarity. When you are centered on yourself, you can set the energy towards what you want to accomplish, whether it's having a project go smoothly or as simple as having great interactions wherever you go.

You are the master of your life, create it wisely!

Setting Intentions

It is important to go through a checklist before you set intentions. In addition, it is ideal to be aware of your thoughts and emotions so that you are in optimal energy in mind and body before you begin. The checklist may include, but is not limited to:

1. Process what you are feeling
2. Acknowledge what memories come up
3. Clear your mind
4. Breathe and Relax
5. Make a list of intentions
6. Feel into what you are creating
7. Be confident and powerful
8. Passionately work towards your goals
9. Be patient
10. Trust the process!

Step Into Your Fullest Potential

Embrace your vibrant self. Start each day with enthusiasm and enjoy living. Do the things you've always wanted to do. Plan your future while being present in the moment and happy. Enjoy every step of your journey. When you show up expecting great things to happen, then that's what you will experience. Remember, life is a dance.

Be Bold, Be Powerful, Be You!

CHAPTER SEVEN

Melissa Porterfield
Silk Mountain
Founder and CEO

www.silkmtn.com
https://facebook.com/silkmtn.com
www.linkedin.com/in/melissa-porterfield

After 20+ years in corporate HR leadership, Melissa founded Silk Mountain. Her firm helps startups build positive, people-first cultures that attract and retain top talent. She coaches executives and their leadership teams to tackle challenges and support highly engaging work environments.

Melissa is an advisor and coach focused on helping clients grow personally and professionally. While continuing her strategic HR work with businesses, she also creates coaching programs that blend life and work. Her upcoming *Hot Mess Minimalism®*, launching in 2025, will offer practical tools to simplify routines, reduce stress, and bring more balance, clarity, and peace of mind to daily life.

A published author and speaker, Melissa has been featured in media outlets, from podcasts to TV. She holds an MEd in Educational Leadership and her Coaching, Human Synergistics®, and MBTI® certifications.

Melissa lives in a historic area of Houston with her musician husband and two dogs.

Never Ask Why

By Melissa Porterfield

Have you ever had a dream so vivid and so real that it jolted you awake? It happened to me just once, many years ago, but that dream turned out to be a game-changer for my personal life and my coaching practice.

Looking back, it all started when I was a teacher many years ago. I've always loved working one-on-one with people, and I found my true passion when our school district began decentralizing its decision-making processes. I was asked to chair the Personnel Committee, a role I landed largely because of my summer job at a staffing agency, which gave me credibility in the eyes of the school's administrators.

That opportunity turned into something transformative. I made key changes that improved the hiring process. One of the most impactful was a simple but crucial shift: Teachers would interview candidates for their qualifications and potential fit within the team. Previously, interviews were handled solely by school administrators, and candidates were assigned to teams based on open positions. This initiative included training teachers on how to interview and holding panel interviews to increase efficiency and consistency.

I didn't stop there. I launched a mentoring program for new teachers, knowing from research that many would leave the profession within their first two years. I had no formal mentoring training at the time, but I threw myself into it. And here's where I stumbled onto something powerful: I found that the most rewarding part of mentoring wasn't telling them what to do, although I enjoyed sharing suggestions based on experience—it was asking them the right questions, questions that led them to solutions they could own. I didn't realize it then, but I did more coaching than mentoring.

Fast-forward to 1999, when I left my role as an assistant principal to become a human resources manager in the corporate world. I continued to work one-on-one with people, but now, my clients were leaders at all levels of the organization. The questions I asked remained a core tool for success. Through coaching conversations, I helped them unlock insights and overcome challenges, just as I had done with my mentees in education.

As I deepened my coaching expertise and became certified, I discovered that the questions I had been asking all along were actually "powerful questions"—a cornerstone of effective coaching. Little did I know how much these questions would shape my future.

In 2017, after being laid off from my last corporate role, I took the plunge and launched Silk Mountain, a strategic HR advisory firm. My focus was clear: help startups and small businesses design their ideal cultures before they start hiring or, when necessary, redefine a dysfunctional culture. At the heart of everything I did was coaching—especially coaching leaders to navigate challenges, change behaviors, and create thriving work environments.

In 2021, I expanded my coaching offerings to include two new programs: one for career coaching, which helps clients land new roles or advance in their current careers, and another for supporting women in identifying and overcoming obstacles like procrastination, perfectionism, and self-doubt.

Circling back to the dream from years ago that I mentioned earlier, I was talking with a friend I knew well. We enthusiastically discussed a range of topics. As our conversation neared its end, he gave me a piece of advice that has stuck with me ever since: "Never ask why."

At first, I was a bit confused. Why wouldn't I ask "why"? He explained that people answer the "why" question through their own personal filters, often with defensiveness or blame. The better approach, he advised, is to ask more specific questions that can get to the root cause—questions like "What," "When," "How," and "Who."

I immediately put this advice into practice with a newly promoted manager I was coaching. She shared a frustrating story: She had asked one of her direct reports for some data to include in an important presentation, but he sent her the wrong information at the last minute. Of course, this made her furious—she couldn't get the correct data in time for the meeting.

Now, if I had asked her, "Why did he do that?" I was pretty sure her response would've been something like, "Because he's a jerk!" or "Because he wants me to fail." She was new in her role, and the situation played into her insecurities, so instead of diving straight into a "why" question, I empathized with her frustration and asked, "What do you think happened?"

She fired back, "He's a jerk! He did it on purpose to make me look bad!"

I didn't react to her anger. Instead, I kept the focus on understanding the situation more fully. I asked her:

- **How do you know that's true?**

- **When has he behaved like this before?**

- **When did you ask him for the data?**

- **What else did he have going on that day?**

- **How has he been to work before this incident?**

I could see her calm down with each question as she reflected on her answers. Slowly, she began to question her assumptions and opened up to the possibility that her colleague wasn't, in fact, a "jerk."

By the end of our session, we had shifted from problem identification to solution-building. I asked her, "What can you do differently to ensure this doesn't happen again?" She immediately began crafting an action plan, energized by the clarity she had gained.

Ultimately, she resolved the issue with her team member and discovered he wasn't a jerk after all—a huge win for her and their working relationship. As for me, I realized just how effective this approach had been and how easy it was to implement. It's been a powerful tool in my coaching toolkit ever since.

If you're not using this method in your coaching practice, I encourage you to give it a try and see the difference, not asking why makes for **your** clients **and** increases your success as a coach!

CHAPTER EIGHT

Shea Collins
365 Mentoring and Coaching, LLC
CEO, President

http://365mentoringandcoaching.carrd.co
www.facebook.com/365MentoringCoaching
www.instagram.com/365_mentoringcoaching

Shea Collins, CAA, M.Ed., CEO of 365 Mentoring and Coaching, LLC, is a dynamic Academic Leader and Career Coach dedicated to guiding students and professionals towards success. Shea's diverse roles include teacher,Girls Basketball Coach, Athletic Administrator, and a proud Virginia State University Alumna.

In addition to being a Certified Athletic Administrator and DEI presenter, Shea's impactful contributions extend to the Virginia Interscholastic Athletic Administrators Association (VIAAA), National Interscholastic Athletic Administrators Association (NIAAA), Virginia High School League (VHSL) and a member of various other communities and committees to include the Global Community of Women in High School Sports that reflects an inclusive and supportive sports environment.

Currently serving as President of the VIAAA, being involved in athletics, which is a critical space for students where the goal is to foster effective students and leaders on and off the court or field. Empowering other leaders through mentorship and coaching has been insightful and impactful to watch our clients soar.

Connect with Shea to embark on a transformative, creative and aspiring journey of personal and professional growth for adults and students.

The Success Coaching Paradigm

By Shea Collins

In today's interconnected world, the path to success rarely runs in isolation. The most effective success coaching can emerge from deep-rooted relationships, creative thinking, and strategic partnerships that amplify both individual and collective potential. Mentorship, partnerships, and collaboration form the foundation of professional and personal growth in today's interconnected world. Through mentorship, experienced individuals share their knowledge, insights, and lessons learned, helping guide others along their journey while avoiding common pitfalls. Partnerships create mutually beneficial relationships where organizations and individuals can combine their unique strengths, resources, and perspectives to achieve goals that would be difficult to accomplish alone. Collaboration takes this concept further by bringing diverse groups together to solve complex problems, fostering innovation through the cross-pollination of ideas and approaches.

Whether in business, academia, or personal development, these relationships create powerful learning ecosystems where knowledge flows freely, challenges are tackled collectively, and success is shared among all participants. This chapter explores how coaches at all levels can leverage the power of mentorships, creative collaboration, and community partnerships to transform their practice and finished products into exceptional value for their clients. This chapter is focused on understanding how mentorships, collaborative teamwork, and partnerships allow not only the business and career coach to achieve success, but also their clients to benefit from those resources and partnerships.

The Mentor's Multiplier Effect

Success coaching transcends the traditional one-on-one dynamic when mentorship becomes its cornerstone. Experienced mentors bring not only their expertise but also their network, insights, and creative wisdom to the coaching relationship. They serve as bridges between theory and practice, helping clients navigate real-world challenges with proven strategies.

Do you know a successful business or career coach who has begun their business and has continued to operate without collaboration or mentorship? Those whom I know and who have mentored me were once mentored, work with others to deliver a finished product, and have used those same relationships to embark on new opportunities. These seasoned professionals can offer invaluable perspectives to their clients, sharing stories of both triumphs and failures. The result is a rich learning environment where clients can access multiple viewpoints and experiences, accelerating their growth and understanding.

Creative Collaboration: Breaking It Down

Creativity flourishes in environments where diverse perspectives intersect. Success coaches who embrace creative collaboration often discover innovative solutions that wouldn't emerge in isolation.

Using this approach to collaboration involves:

- Building interdisciplinary networks that bring together professionals from different fields
- Facilitating and constructing structured brainstorming sessions
- Creating safe spaces for experimental thinking and calculated risk-taking

- Encouraging clients to step outside their comfort zones and engage with new perspectives

Working in these collaborative spaces creates a more creative expression, unlocking new ways of thinking about an idea or project, how to organize and think about one's professional goals, and how to overcome any limits that one has set for oneself.

The Power of Local Partnerships

Community partnerships represent an often-untapped resource for success coaches. Local organizations, businesses, and institutions can provide:

- Real-world learning laboratories for clients and access to specialized resources and facilities

- Networking opportunities and potential mentors

- Practical application of coaching concepts

When one navigates entrepreneurial space as a career, business, or success, establishing partnerships and a network is essential to building your brand. Creating time to seek partnerships with some of the various groups below can help create a network of often silent yet powerful individuals.

Consider some of the following groups to partner with. These partnerships create a robust ecosystem that supports client growth and development. They also provide coaches with continuous learning opportunities and exposure to emerging trends and challenges in various sectors.

1. Local Chambers of Commerce

2. Small Business Development Centers

3. Community Colleges and Universities

4. Industry-specific Professional Associations

5. Nonprofit Organizations

6. Co-working Spaces and Innovation Hubs

Creating Synergistic Value: Putting it All Together

Success coaches who master the art of resource integration can offer their clients unprecedented value. This involves using knowledge resources, physical resources, human resources, technology platforms, and client success.

Knowledge Resources

- Developing shared learning platforms
- Creating collaborative content libraries
- Establishing mentor databases
- Professional learning communities
- Physical Resources
- Sharing workspace and meeting facilities
- Creating collaborative learning environments
- Community impact and activities

Human Resources

- Building networks of subject matter experts
- Creating mentor pools and developing peer support groups

- Establishing professional communities
- The Technology Platforms
- Digital collaboration tools for virtual mentoring sessions
- Online learning management systems for resource sharing
- Social media platforms for community building
- Virtual and other remote partnership meetings

Implementation & Strategery

Success coaches can implement these collaborative approaches through a structured process. The implementation and structure that individual coaches create will not be an overnight success. However, with a plan in place (that may change over time), success, business, and career coaches can create programs using the following phases to ensure the success of their clients and platforms.

1. Assessment Phase

    - Evaluate current resources and capabilities
    - Identify potential partnership opportunities
    - Analyze client needs and preferences
    - Review community resources and gaps

2. Planning Phase

    - Develop partnership strategies
    - Create resource integration plans

- Design collaborative programs and establish measurement criteria

3. Implementation Phase

- Launch pilot programs
- Build partnership relationships
- Integrate new resources
- Train team members and partners

4. Evaluation Phase

- Measure outcomes
- Gather feedback and adjust strategies
- Scale successful initiatives

Future Trends

The future of success coaching through creative collaboration and partnerships has changed. With the advancement of technology to include online platforms and digital resources, with limited brick-and-mortar locations, coaches must adjust to the changes. The future of coaching has caused those navigating the coaching world to embrace the following:

- Artificial Intelligence (AI) integration for personalized coaching
- Virtual reality platforms for immersive learning
- Global partnership networks
- Enhanced data analytics for measuring impact

Conclusion

Success coaching through creative collaboration, mentorship, and partnerships represents a powerful approach to achieving exceptional results. By leveraging mentorship, combining resources, and building strategic partnerships, coaches can create comprehensive support systems that enhance client success while building sustainable practices. While leveraging this impact, it should not take away the human nature that is needed when dealing with clients.

The key to success lies in remaining flexible, open to innovation, and committed to continuous improvement. As you develop your collaborative coaching practice, remember that every partnership and creative initiative should align with your core mission: helping clients achieve their full potential. Remember, every client does not have the same goals, missions, and desired outcomes. Tailoring your programs and client services to fit the needs of those you serve will create more opportunities for impact.

Through the thoughtful integration of these elements, successful coaches can build practices that not only serve their clients more effectively but also contribute to the broader professional community. Building a professional community should not feel like work. Using the various networks and others in the profession creates a widespread effect. The future of coaching lies not in isolation but in the powerful synergies created through creative collaboration and strategic partnerships. Let's continue to build our platforms and be innovative while creating unlimited growth potential for you and your clients.

CHAPTER NINE

Sonja Sells
Sonja Sells Enterprises LLC & Chakelet Drap Inspired LLC
Founder

www.sonjasells.com
www.instagram.com/sonjasells
www.linkedin.com/in/sonjasells
www.facebook.com/sonjasellsenterprises

Sonja Sells ignites a revolution for women 35+, liberating them from suffocating routines to build thriving online businesses. A Business Empowerment Growth Strategist and serial entrepreneur, she champions financial and lifestyle freedom, driven by her transformative journey. In 2017, navigating an identity crisis under a rigid schedule, Sonja embarked on a path of self-discovery. Serving as Executive Assistant to high-performing entrepreneurs, including those at a $21B pharmaceutical giant, she gained invaluable insights into successful business operations and the power of overcoming personal roadblocks. This pivotal period ignited her fire, fueling her mission to empower others.

Her signature Break Free. Be Fierce. Transformation Program, delivered through Sonja Sells Enterprises LLC, and powered by the T.I.M.E. Framework—Truth, Ignite, Momentum, Empower—guides women through a visceral journey of self-discovery.

Leveraging her hard-earned experience, Sonja equips women with the tools and strategies to scale thriving online businesses. Her mission: to empower women to "break free and be fierce," unlocking their inherent potential for abundance.

Beyond Sonja Sells Enterprises LLC, her influence extends through Chakelet Drap Inspired LLC, providing accessible personal and professional development resources. "The Sonja Empowers Show" podcast delivers weekly actionable strategies and inspiration. As an empowerment speaker, coach, and author, she distills complex business ideas into digestible, transformative strategies, empowering women to design lives of purpose and prosperity.

Connect with her on YouTube, Instagram, and LinkedIn @ SonjaSells. Explore more at SonjaSells.com and ChakeletDrapInspired.com.

Break Free. Be Fierce.: A Framework for Women Entrepreneurs

By Sonja Sells

Have you ever felt the weight of the world pressing down on your shoulders? The crushing weight of self-doubt, the gnawing fear of failure, the constant comparison to others that leaves you feeling inadequate? I know that feeling intimately. I remember nights spent staring at the ceiling, tears tracing paths down my face, wondering if I was strong enough, talented enough, worthy enough.

I was trapped in a cycle of self-sabotage, constantly battling the voices in my head that whispered doubts and limitations. 'You're not good enough.' 'You'll never succeed.' 'Who do you think you are?' These insidious thoughts held me captive, preventing me from even attempting to fly.

But then, a flicker of defiance ignited within me—a refusal to surrender to the narrative of my own self-destruction. I began to question the validity of those voices, challenging the assumptions holding me back. I realized that my biggest obstacle wasn't the competition, the market, or the economy. It was the negative self-talk, the limiting beliefs I had unconsciously embraced.

This is where the journey of self-discovery truly begins. It's about unearthing the limiting beliefs that are holding you back, those deeply ingrained patterns of thought that whisper doubts and sabotage your efforts. It's about recognizing that your power lies within, not in external validation or the approval of others.

Ignite the Fire Within means recognizing your inherent worth, embracing your unique talents, and cultivating a mindset of unwavering self-belief. It's about silencing the inner critic and replacing those negative voices with affirmations of strength, courage, and resilience.

This isn't about becoming someone else; it's about uncovering the authentic you, the woman who dares to dream big, refuses to settle for less, and is ready to ignite her revolution.

The T.I.M.E. Framework is your guide to unlocking the "Fire Within" – that inner spark of passion, drive, and resilience that lies dormant within each of us. It's about tapping into your unique strengths, overcoming your fears, and creating a life of purpose and fulfillment.

Let's delve into each pillar of the T.I.M.E. Framework that will equip you to thrive:

T is for Truth

The foundation of any successful endeavor rests on truth. And for women entrepreneurs, this truth begins with embracing our authentic selves. Shed the layers of societal expectations and the pressure to conform. Embrace the unique, vibrant woman you are with all your quirks, passions, and vulnerabilities. Your authenticity is your superpower, attracting customers who resonate with your genuine spirit.

Break Free. Be Fierce. Strategies:

- **Self-Reflection Exercises:** Journaling prompts focused on identifying core values, passions, and unique strengths. Explore past experiences where authenticity led to positive outcomes.
- **Authenticity Audits:** Review marketing materials, brand messaging, and client interactions to ensure alignment with the

true self. Identify areas where presenting a "polished" version overshadows genuine personality.

- **Community Building:** Connect with other women entrepreneurs who champion authenticity. Share stories and challenges related to being true to oneself in business.

Confronting our fears is another crucial aspect of this truth. Fear, in all its forms – fear of failure, fear of judgment, fear of the unknown – seeks to extinguish the inner fire that fuels our entrepreneurial spirit. But within that fear lies a powerful truth: your potential is limitless. Face your fears head-on, not with bravado, but with courage and a deep understanding of your own strength.

Break Free. Be Fierce. Strategies:

- **Fear Mapping:** Identify specific fears and analyze their root causes. Challenge the validity of those fears with logic and evidence.

- **"What's the Worst That Could Happen?" Exercise:** Walk through scenarios of potential failures to reduce their perceived impact. Develop contingency plans to mitigate risks.

- **Small Steps Approach:** Break down large, daunting goals into smaller, manageable tasks to build confidence and momentum. Celebrate each milestone achieved.

Finally, listen deeply to the whispers of feedback. Feedback, both positive and constructive, is a mirror reflecting your strengths and weaknesses. Listen not to criticize but to learn. Like a piece of coal, each piece of feedback can fuel your fire and help you refine your path.

Break Free. Be Fierce. Strategies:

- **Feedback Framework:** Develop a structured approach to receiving and processing feedback. Focus on identifying actionable insights and separating personal opinions from constructive criticism.

- **Seek Diverse Perspectives:** Actively solicit feedback from clients, mentors, peers, and even competitors to gain a well-rounded understanding of your performance.

- **Implement and Iterate:** Prioritize feedback that aligns with your values and business goals. Track the impact of implemented changes and adjust your approach as needed.

I is for Ignite

Igniting your entrepreneurial journey requires a deep connection to your passion. What sets your soul on fire? What problems keep you awake at night, yearning for a solution? Connect with that deep-seated passion, that burning desire to make a difference. It's the fuel that will sustain you through the inevitable challenges.

Break Free. Be Fierce. Strategies:

- **Passion Discovery:** Explore different industries, hobbies, and social issues to identify what truly resonates. Reflect on past experiences that evoked strong feelings of purpose and fulfillment.

- **Problem-Solving Focus:** Identify problems you are passionate about solving. Research existing solutions and brainstorm innovative approaches.

- **Vision Boarding:** Create a visual representation of your ideal future, incorporating images and words that evoke your passions and goals.

Paint a vivid picture of your success. Close your eyes and envision your business thriving, your impact resonating, and your dreams becoming a reality. This vivid picture will guide your every decision and inspire you to persevere through the toughest times.

Break Free. Be Fierce. Strategies:

- **Visualization Exercises:** Regularly practice visualizing your desired outcomes, focusing on the specific details of your success.
- **Affirmations:** Develop positive affirmations that reinforce your belief in your ability to achieve your goals. Repeat these affirmations daily.
- **Goal Setting:** Set clear, measurable, achievable, relevant, and time-bound (SMART) goals that align with your vision.

Embrace the growth within you. Every challenge, every setback, is an opportunity for growth. Embrace the discomfort and the uncertainty. These are the fertile grounds where your greatest strengths will blossom.

Break Free. Be Fierce. Strategies:

- **Growth Mindset Development:** Foster a belief that talents and intellect can evolve through commitment and perseverance. Embrace challenges as chances for education and advancement.
- **Resilience Building:** Develop strategies for bouncing back from setbacks. Focus on learning from mistakes and maintaining a positive outlook.
- **Continuous Learning:** Commit to ongoing learning and development through books, courses, and mentorship.

M is for Momentum

Just as a mighty oak needs deep roots, your business needs a strong foundation. Develop a solid vision-based plan, understand your market, and create a compelling value proposition. This foundation will provide the stability you need to weather any storm.

Break Free. Be Fierce. Strategies:

- **Business Plan Development:** Create a vision-based plan that outlines your vision, mission, target market, and financial projections.
- **Market Research:** Conduct thorough market research to understand your target audience and their needs.
- **Value Proposition Design:** Clearly articulate your unique value to your customers and how you differentiate yourself.

Momentum is not a destination; it's a continuous flow. Take consistent, decisive action, even when you feel overwhelmed. Celebrate small victories, and let each accomplishment fuel your drive to achieve even greater things.

Break Free. Be Fierce. Strategies:

- **Time Management Techniques:** Implement effective time management strategies to prioritize tasks, manage distractions, and stay focused on your goals.
- **Progress Tracking:** Track your progress regularly and celebrate milestones achieved. This will help you stay motivated and maintain momentum.
- **Systems:** Streamline recurring tasks with repeatable systems and processes. This reduces decision fatigue and ensures consistency, freeing you to focus on growth.

You don't have to do this alone. Surround yourself with a network of supportive women–mentors, peers, and friends. Share your journey, seek their guidance, and celebrate their successes.

Break Free. Be Fierce. Strategies:

- **Networking:** Actively participate in networking events and online communities to connect with other women entrepreneurs.
- **Mentorship:** Seek mentors who can provide guidance and support based on their experiences.
- **Accountability Partners:** Partner with other entrepreneurs to provide mutual support and accountability.

E is for Empower

This journey is not just about building a successful business; it's about empowering yourself to become the best version of yourself. Empowering yourself means pushing beyond your perceived limitations. It's about investing in your growth, developing new skills, and stepping outside your comfort zone.

Break Free. Be Fierce. Strategies:

- **Skills Assessment:** Identify areas where you need to develop new skills to achieve your business goals.
- **Personal Development Plan:** Create a plan for personal and professional development, including courses, workshops, and other learning opportunities.
- **Embrace Discomfort:** Actively seek opportunities to step outside your comfort zone and challenge yourself.

When you empower yourself, you reignite the passion and drive that fuels your entrepreneurial journey. This is your time. This is your journey. Ignite your inner fire, embrace your power, and create a future that reflects your deepest aspirations. Break free from limitations, be fierce, and unleash the extraordinary woman entrepreneur within.

CHAPTER TEN

Cherie Faus-Smith
Joyful Midlife Misfits
CEO/Empowerment & Joy Coach for Midlife Women/Speaker/Author

https://cheriefaus-smith.com/
https://www.linkedin.com/in/cheriefaus-smith
https://www.facebook.com/cherie.faus.smith

Meet Cherie Faus-Smith, a passionate coach and Chief Joy Misfit on a mission to empower women to embrace their unique journeys. With a heart full of empathy and a knack for turning challenges into triumphs, Cherie specializes in helping women navigate the beautiful chaos of midlife with confidence and joy. After overcoming her own misdiagnosis of agoraphobia and discovering her personality as a Highly Sensitive Person (HSP), she now thrives on guiding others to celebrate their quirks and redefine success on their own terms. When she's not coaching, you can find her dancing like nobody's watching, hanging out in a local cat café, sipping coffee and socializing with the kitties, and hugging a tree. Join Cherie in celebrating the magic of misfits and unlocking the extraordinary potential within every woman!

The Joyful Midlife Misfit: Embracing Sensitivity and Authenticity for Success

By Cherie Faus-Smith

I always knew I was different. As a child, I was the one who felt deeply, too deeply, some said. The sound of an argument could linger in my chest for hours. The glare of fluorescent lights in a classroom felt like needles piercing my skin. I was labeled "overly sensitive," told to "toughen up," and often felt like I didn't fit the mold of what the world expected.

But the real turning point came years later, in midlife, when I found myself sitting in a doctor's office, clutching a diagnosis that felt like a punch to the gut: agoraphobia. The word alone sent me spiraling. Was I broken? Was there something fundamentally wrong with me? I had always avoided overly stimulating environments - crowded shopping malls, loud parties - but surely that didn't make me incapable of functioning in the world.

I left that office feeling lost, questioning everything about who I was. What I didn't know at the time was that this misdiagnosis would become the catalyst for my transformation. It was the beginning of a journey that led me to uncover a truth that changed my life: I wasn't broken. I was an HSP—a Highly Sensitive Person. And that sensitivity, which I once viewed as a weakness, would become my superpower.

The Birth of a Joyful Midlife Misfit

Discovering I was an HSP felt like finding the missing piece of a puzzle I had been trying to solve my entire life. It explained why I needed alone time to recharge after social events, why I noticed details others overlooked, and why I felt emotions so intensely. But it wasn't just about understanding myself; it was about learning to celebrate the very traits I had spent years suppressing.

This realization didn't come easily. Society often tells us to conform, to fit into neat little boxes that define success. But as I ventured deeper into my self-discovery, I realized I wasn't meant to fit into any box. I was a joyful midlife misfit - someone who thrives by embracing the parts of herself that don't conform to traditional expectations.

And the more I shared my journey, the more I learned I wasn't alone. I began connecting with other women who felt like misfits in their own lives - women who were tired of trying to fit in and ready to embrace their unique paths.

Lessons for Joyful Midlife Misfits

As a joyful midlife misfit, I've learned that life doesn't have to look like anyone else's version of success in order to be deeply meaningful. The lessons I'm about to share with you aren't just lessons I've uncovered for myself - they've become the very foundation of my work with other women who feel like they, too, don't fit into society's narrow expectations.

Here's what I've learned about thriving as a joyful midlife misfit:

1. **Authenticity is Magnetic**

   - When you show up as your true self, you attract the right people, opportunities, and experiences. Pretending to be someone you're not only leads to frustration and burnout. When I embraced my sensitivity and learned to lean into my quirks, I found the kind of connections and opportunities I had always longed for.

2. **Sensitivity is a Superpower**

    - For years, I saw my sensitivity as a burden. I believed it made life harder, so I tried to suppress it. But I've learned that sensitivity is my greatest strength. It allows me to connect deeply with others, notice nuances, and bring empathy into everything I do. And this is what the world needs - more sensitive, compassionate people. If you're an HSP, your sensitivity is not a flaw - it's your superpower. Honor it, protect it, and let it guide you.

3. **Joy Comes from Alignment**

    - True joy isn't about checking off society's boxes; it's about aligning your actions with your values and passions. For me, that meant embracing midlife as a time of reinvention, not decline. When you stop chasing external validation and instead focus on what feels right for you, joy becomes a natural byproduct.

4. **Your "Too Much" is Just Enough**

    - I spent most of my life being told I was "too sensitive," "too emotional," or "too loud." I internalized those messages, believing they were flaws. But I've come to understand that what others perceive as "too much" is exactly what makes me unique. If you've ever been told you're too much or not enough, hear me when I say this: You're just the right amount of everything you need to be.

5. **Success Can Be Redefined on Your Terms**

    - Success doesn't have to look like a corner office or a six-figure salary. It can look like joyfully pursuing your passions, building meaningful relationships, or simply waking up each day feeling aligned with your purpose. When you let go of society's rigid definitions of success, you create space to define what it means for you. For me, success is about helping other women embrace their unique power and potential.

Practical Tools for Thriving as a Misfit

Being a joyful midlife misfit doesn't happen overnight. It takes intentionality and care. Here are a few strategies I've developed for myself and my clients to thrive in a world that often prizes conformity:

- **Set Boundaries:** As an HSP, protecting your energy is essential. Learn to say no to things that drain you and yes to things that light you up.

- **Practice Self-Compassion:** Let go of the need to be perfect. Embrace your quirks, flaws, and imperfections - they're exactly what make you beautifully human.

- **Find Your Tribe:** Surround yourself with people who celebrate your uniqueness and lift you up. Your misfit qualities are your superpower, and the right people will recognize that.

- **Lean Into Joy:** Life is too short to live by someone else's rules. Find what brings you joy - whether it's painting, gardening, traveling, or simply spending time with loved ones - and make it a priority.

A Call to Embrace Your Inner Misfit

If there's one thing I want you to take away from this chapter, it's this: being a joyful midlife misfit isn't about fitting in - it's about standing out. It's about embracing the parts of yourself that make you different and using them to create a life that feels authentic and fulfilling.

Midlife isn't the end of the road; it's a powerful new beginning. It's a time to shed expectations that no longer serve you, to step into your true self, and to live with joy, purpose, and unapologetic authenticity.

So here's my invitation to you: stop trying to fit into the mold. Instead, break the mold. Embrace your inner misfit, lean into your sensitivity, and redefine success on your own terms. You're not too much. You're not too sensitive. You're exactly who you're meant to be. And the world needs you - just as you are.

CHAPTER ELEVEN

Emily South
Truevoice, LLC
CEO / Transformative Coach / Speaker

http://findyourtruevoice.com/
https://www.linkedin.com/in/emily-south/
https://www.instagram.com/emiique/
https://www.facebook.com/emiisouth/

Emily South is founder of Truevoice, best-selling author, certified queer transformational coach, and keynote speaker passionate about empowering others to live their truest, most authentic, brave, and expansive lives. She helps entrepreneurs find their true voice and be seen for who they truly are, so they can feel confident in all situations.

With 20 years of experience as an entrepreneur, digital marketing consultant, corporate trainer, and leadership coaching, she helps clients achieve breakthroughs at the crossroads of personal and professional life. Emily South is a sought-after international speaker who has inspired audiences worldwide to be mindful, authentic, and wholehearted in relationships, the spaces we embody, and life.

Emily takes an integrated, holistic approach to coaching. She created the S.P.A.C.E. Method, blending both Western and Eastern spiritual practices, science, neuroscience, and quantum physics to support her clients' goals to let go of fears, release limiting beliefs, and take inspired action to manifest their dreams.

Emily is a 5x certified coach in mindset, identity, NLP, EFT, and hypnosis, and thinks outside the box. She firmly believes the way forward for humanity is integration and alignment, plus embracing diversity and equity for all. Together we rise!

Creating Space: The Authentic Coach's Method

By Emily South

The Wake-Up Call

The calendar alert chimed again—my fifth back-to-back coaching session was about to begin, my first book deadline loomed, the website was still under construction, and three social media posts needed attention by day's end. I smiled at my client through the screen, but inside, I was drowning. I had become the coach who couldn't practice what she preached.

That night, I was on my daily walk under the stars, thinking about my journey from hiding my true identity to stepping into the spotlight as a model, then an actress, then a consultant, and now a coach. The most powerful transformation in my life hadn't come from saying 'yes' to everything—it came from creating space to hear my authentic voice. The same voice that had whispered for years that I was a woman, despite what the world told me.

I realized then that I was teaching my clients to find what I call their "true voice" while simultaneously drowning out my own with an overcrowded calendar and constant digital noise. The next morning, I reconnected to my voice, canceled three commitments, blocked off two hours for meditation, and began developing what would become my S.P.A.C.E. Method, the core principles of my A.I.C.C. (Authentic Integrated Conscious Creator) coaching program.

The Modern Challenge

Ever feel like there's no space for YOU on your calendar? What if you could turn your FOMO into your secret weapon to curate your dream life and empower your coaching clients to do the same?"

In this modern AI world, there is an endless supply of distractions and opportunities to create a meaningful impact. It's more important than ever to create space first for self and others. How can we show up for and be relevant to our clients in a way that is empowering and still have the time and energy for our personal and professional growth and expansion? The way forward is to integrate, not segregate, our parts as a society, and I believe the S.P.A.C.E. Method is part of that future. This will help us all heal, grow, find our own true voice, and rise together!

The S.P.A.C.E. Method

As I completed my coaching certifications and started creating the A.I.C.C. program, I reflected on how essential it is to create space for the journey of self-discovery and transformation to unfold in mind, body, and soul. This led me to develop the S.P.A.C.E. Method, a structured, multi-level progression that can be applied simultaneously or continuously in personal and coaching relationships. The foundational elements include:

- S -- Be a Safe space for all with mutual love and respect.
- P -- Be fully in the Present moment, free from distractions.
- A -- Be Authentic, meaning speak your truth and hold space for others too.
- C -- Be Curious and ask questions (differences will arise as opportunities to learn)
- E -- Only Empowering exchanges are allowed in the space. What we feel, we create!

The S.P.A.C.E. Method expands into two additional levels for personal mastery and advanced integrations and is designed to create environments where transformation can flourish - both for coaches and clients alike. Feel free to inquire about upcoming certifications.

For example, one of my clients was able to reconnect with parts of herself she hadn't fully integrated, a childhood memory, and release generational fear she'd been carrying around for decades. She looked and felt happier, more aligned, and noticed improvements in her sleep and overall well-being.

My Journey to S.P.A.C.E.

This acronym has its origins in my coming out story. Coming out was inevitable but how I showed up in the process was revolutionary. For example, I choose to create a space for myself independent from others. The peace I felt knowing my true voice grounded me as my life was falling apart. It protected me as I was cut off from family, friends, and my church and estranged from my four children. Instead of caving into the identity crisis and trauma, I tried modeling for 2 years and acting for 4.5 years, which opened me to new people, spaces, and opportunities to grow. I stayed curious through the process and found my new tribe. I was led to the higher consciousness community and mindfulness. I learned how to love both the light and the shadow aspects and reconnect with my intuition. I shifted from burnout to boundaries with a therapist, adopted daily self-care rituals, shedding old identities and stories. I dropped the people-pleasing, perfectionism, and performance culture and discovered peace of mind.

Next, I found a life coach who helped me release fears, doubts, and limiting beliefs by teaching me how to reprogram my subconscious mind and take back my power as a conscious creator in my own life. Investing in myself was the smartest decision I've made so far. Today,

I am a certified coach in mindset, identity, NLP (Neural Linguistic Programming), EFT (Emotional Freedom Technique), and hypnosis.

Coming out was an incredible journey of awakening, and it has led me to use a holistic integrated approach, blending both ancient and modern spiritual practices with science, neuroscience, and quantum physics to empower my clients to find their true voice and live brave, bold, authentic, and balanced lives.

The Fundamental Truth

I've meditated on how to honor my true voice and share the S.P.A.C.E. Method with the world, and my intuition and the universe kept pointing me back to a singular truth:

"Our capacity to create space for others is proportional to our ability and capacity to create space for ourselves."

The hermetic teaching "As above so below, as within so without" teaches the same concept of the world reflecting back who you are. You can't give what you don't have. As coaches, self-care and self-love practices are non-negotiable. This means we block out our time, energy, and resources for our growth and expansion with adequate space between clients so we can rest, reflect, refocus, and realign. Setting boundaries is essential to prevent burnout, avoid resentment, find a sense of balance, increase self-respect, and improve the client-coach relationship. As you invest in yourself and keep your commitments, your capacity and confidence will grow. Be clear, firm, concise, and direct with others to protect your time and energy. List your most important priorities, listen to and follow your intuition, practice saying "no," use I-statements, avoid apologies, be consistent, expect discomfort, remember daily gratitude, stay calm, be respectful but confident, visualize the positive outcomes, take time for yourself, and be honest with what time you can commit to.

Business Essentials

Be intentional about all aspects of your business and learn to delegate – the entity structure, mission, values, marketing, products, services, and team – to support the well-being of all parties involved so you don't burn out.

Top 5 Business Essentials:

- Mission statement – Includes your WHY statement, values, and target audience
- Code of ethics – Guidelines to ensure the team is aligned with ethics, professionalism, and the way you run your business.
- Client agreement & disclosure statement – Establish the scope of practice and integrity.
- Client intake form – Initial client questionnaire to establish baseline and background information for all services.
- CRM – Customer Relationship Management to store and protect client data.

The success of your coaching business hinges on two elements – your personal brand and your WHY:

The personal brand comes from who you are and what makes you unique – decide who the fuck you are and be unapologetic – what makes you different is your superpower, often forged in the fires of your healing and/or awakening journey. Sometimes, the answers we seek come to us through us and light the way for all. What if you stepped into being 100% you, spoke your truth from the heart, and it changed the world?

The WHY behind your desire to coach needs to have some soul. What specifically lights you up about guiding others? Don't just echo the gurus and make bank – that ain't gonna cut it. What's your "WHY," your core purpose, the fire within your soul that sustains you to guide others? This needs to be the bedrock of your coaching practice, the unwavering force that keeps you grounded, fuels massive impact, and connects to your authentic voice. What if your "WHY" was so powerful it drowned out all the noise and kept you laser-focused on your unique mission?

Daily S.P.A.C.E. Practices

- Morning rituals – affirmations, grounding, meditation, and journaling to set intentions.
- Daily movement – walks, yoga, hiking, tai chi, qigong, or cardio
- Daily sunlight – 5-10 minutes for vitamin D, mood boost, and serotonin
- Breathwork – box breathing 4-4-4-4
- EFT tapping – helps to release emotions and activate energy centers of the body (chakras)
- Solfeggio or binaural beats – help to reduce stress and boost mood
- Subliminals – realign your thoughts, feelings, and beliefs with your highest self.

Once we know how to create space, we can visit the stories that others placed on us, the stories we co-created, and become mindful of the limiting beliefs that come from these. This in turns gives us the awareness, courage, and compassion to decide if these are empowering or disempowering stories or beliefs. Ask yourself – do they add value to my life? If not, let go and create new ones.

Your Authentic Power

"Your time is limited, so don't waste it living someone else's life... Don't let the noise of others' opinions drown out your own inner voice."

-Steve Jobs

To my fellow coaches, I say this: Trust your inner knowing or intuition by quieting the mind and listening to the heart. Your story is your strength. Your journey is the message. Your authentic self is your superpower.

Creating space isn't just a technique—it's a transformative practice that reconnects you to your essence and amplifies your impact. When you honor your boundaries and nurture your inner voice, you become a living example of what's possible for your clients. Remember that the most powerful coaching happens not from a place of depletion but from a well of abundance you've intentionally cultivated.

Make S.P.A.C.E. your daily commitment, and watch your life and coaching practice transform from the inside out.

CHAPTER TWELVE

Tiffany Wright
Anthem 816 Home Solutions
CO-Owner/Interior Designer

Anthem816.com
https://www.linkedin.com/in/tiffany-wright-560682358
Anthem 816 Home Solutions

Tiffany Wright is a former preschool owner and educator with over a decade of experience shaping young minds and building strong communities. Her passion for creating intentional, beautiful spaces led her to pivot into real estate redevelopment and investing, where she now loves transforming properties with vision and purpose. Tiffany also brings her creative flair to interior design, helping clients turn houses into homes that reflect both function and personality.

With a unique blend of business savvy, educational insight, and design expertise, Tiffany approaches every project with heart, purpose, and a desire to uplift those around her. Whether leading in the classroom or reimagining a fixer-upper, her mission remains the same: to build something that lasts, to make a difference, and to have a whole lot of fun while she's at it, too.

Tiffany is a proud wife and mom of four, and she believes in the power of faith, family, and being bold.

Success... Yep, That's the Goal

By Tiffany Wright

I don't have it all figured out, I'm learning every single day, just like everyone else. These are simply some of the highlights that have shaped, stretched, and helped me grow. I'm a woman on a mission to be bold in this world. I'm a proud wife, mom, friend, and entrepreneur. Someone who's trying to live with heart, make a meaningful impact, and be intentional about the legacy I leave behind.

What is your definition of Success?

Success is a word that gets thrown around a lot. For some, it means climbing the corporate ladder or building an empire. For others, it's creating art, changing lives, or financial freedom. But for me, when I was a little girl, success meant one thing: having a strong marriage and a close relationship with my kids.

I grew up with a lot of chaos—a very broken home, which meant a lot of hardships along the way, but I always knew I wanted the fairy tale story, my knight in shining armor, the white picket fence, the whole shebang! People always told me, "Tiffany, that just isn't how it is in the real world." But deep down, I knew better. I believed with everything in me that I could have that kind of life. When I was 21; I was lucky enough to find my husband Adam, hands down, the best thing that ever happened to me. I'm proud to say that we have an awesome marriage, life, and family. One that I had always dreamed of! Of course, it's not perfect. We're not perfect. But it's real, and it's rooted in love, faith, and commitment.

We have four beautiful kids that we are beyond proud of. I know this might be cliche, but I mean this from deep down, that our family will always be what I'm most proud of, and part of the legacy I leave behind. Also, I want to mention we have two super cute doggies, and they're pretty awesome, too!

My point is, success looks different for everyone. Even today, while my faith and marriage remain my top priorities, I have audacious goals and dreams for myself and our future.

But no matter what kind of success you're chasing, I do believe there are some important principles that will always apply.

Your Inner Blueprint Matters!

The way we see ourselves shapes everything.

You can set big goals, make vision boards, and read all the personal development books in the world—but if you don't believe it deep in your core, it's never going to stick. Our subconscious minds are running the show more than we realize. Scientists say up to 95% of our daily actions are driven by our subconscious. In fact, according to renowned social psychologist Timothy D. Wilson, he estimates that the subconscious mind processes around 11 million bits of information per second while the conscious mind only processes about 40-50 bits per second! That's a HUGE percent! That means we don't just need to think differently —we need to BELIEVE differently - put this big part of our brains to work… IMMEDIATELY!

It's like having an internal blueprint. You may want to build a mansion of success, but if your subconscious blueprint is a shack, guess what gets built? You have to update the design inside before you can manifest anything outside.

I truly believe we all face trials in this life, and I'm not here to compare scars. But I do know this: whatever beliefs or patterns have shaped your past, they don't have to determine your future. Like the song from The Greatest Showman, "Rewrite the Stars,"

You can rewrite your blueprint. Take control of the narrative you've been handed and shape it into something great. And coming from a woman of faith, I believe we should absolutely bring God into this part of the story. I believe if you have small dreams, God wants to elevate those. I also believe that if you have big dreams, He wants to elevate those too. So have audacious goals. Dream big!

One powerful tool that taps into our subconscious is setting specific goals with clear deadlines. Think about how your brain reacts when you have to catch an early flight or give a big presentation. You probably toss and turn the night before, because your mind is actively preparing. That's your subconscious at work. So when you set a goal, be specific. Write it down. Attach a date. The more detailed and concrete, the more your brain goes to work for you - how powerful is that?

Let's change the internal narrative. You have to see yourself as someone worthy, capable, and already becoming the person you dream of being. And then you have to give that dream a timeline. That's when transformation starts, not just from the outside in, but from the inside out.

Repetition, Repetition, Repetition!

I'm a Texas girl, and in Texas, we're raised on faith, family, freedom, and football. We bleed the red, white, and blue. We love our country, and we love our sports teams. Hook 'em Horns! So I'm gonna have some sports references, because the way I see it, we always want to be learning from the experts - the best of the best!

Greatness isn't built on talent alone. It's built on what you do when no one's watching. It's built on reps!

Take Steph Curry, for example. Even though he's already one of the greatest shooters of all time, he's known for practicing 500 shots a day. Not because he needs to prove anything—because let's be real, he's already Steph Curry, and he's already going down in history as one of the greatest NBA players of all time. He understands that consistency keeps you sharp. It's what separates the good from the GREAT!

The same principle applies to how we think and speak. Repetition isn't just about physical action—it's also about mental rehearsal. If you want to be a millionaire, have a thriving marriage, or overcome anxiety, you have to repeat the thoughts, words, and actions that match that version of you. You can't just say it once and hope it sticks. You have to say it, see it, believe it —and do it daily!

Science calls this neuroplasticity—the brain's ability to rewire itself. What you repeat, you reinforce. So tell yourself, "I am worthy. I am capable. I am focused. I am blessed. I am disciplined, I am a Millionaire, I am an awesome mom, I am an awesome businesswoman." Say it out loud. Visualize it. Act as if it's already true. Because eventually, your brain catches up to your vision.

Repetition creates habits. Habits create identity. And identity creates destiny.

Success is Built on Trust, Connection, and Service

In today's world, deception is everywhere. Everyone seems to be looking out for themselves, curating perfect lives online while struggling silently behind the scenes. That's why authenticity matters more than ever. Being real, being humble, and loving people over profits is the real key to long-term success.

People can feel when you're genuine. They can sense if you're here to serve or here to take. Poet Ella Wheeler Wilcox captured this best in her poem "Which Are You?"

There are two kinds of people on earth today;

Just two types of people, no more, I say.

Not the sinner and saint....

Not the rich and the poor....

Not the humble and proud....

Not the happy and sad....

No, the two kinds of people on earth, I mean,

Are the people who lift and the people who lean?

So, how do you want to connect with those around you, as someone who gives or someone who takes?

Successful influence with people also requires humility. The greatest people I've studied are always learning and always listening. One of my favorite quotes is from Nick Saban, head coach of Alabama football (also one of the greats). He said, "One of the most important things about leadership is that you have to have the kind of humility that will allow you to be coached."

To be teachable is a huge component of humility and success. I've always believed that sometimes you have a good idea—until you hear a better one.

That mindset has saved me more times than I can count, especially in parenting. Just when I thought I was doing it right... Sure enough, a new problem would arise. One of the things we say in our house is: "If there's a problem, yo, I'll solve it." And what I actually mean is "I'm gonna buy a book!" Because chances are, someone else has been there, figured it out, and written it down. And I want to learn from them.

That willingness to keep learning, to stay humble, and to keep growing—that's what sets people apart.

I can't end without mentioning service! Use your gifts. Give of your time and talents that the good Lord has blessed all of us with! Encourage someone, pray for someone, speak at that event for free, mentor others, call that friend, send that text!!

Service grounds you. It connects you to something bigger. One of my favorite examples of servant leadership is Dabo Swinney, head coach of the Clemson Tigers. Swinney took a team that had struggled for years and transformed it into a national powerhouse, winning championships in 2016 and 2018, including an undefeated 15–0 season. But beyond the wins, it's how he leads that stands out.

Swinney once told his team, "We're going to do things differently. If we show up at another college to play, we're going to leave that locker room cleaner than we found it. No matter where we go, we are going to leave it better than we found it. We do common things in an uncommon way."

That kind of mindset? It's rare. And it's powerful. Because real success isn't just about results—it's about how you achieve them. It's about leaving people, places, and moments better than you found them.

That's the kind of success that changes the world.

Guys, in conclusion - Go and Build it!

You don't need permission to pursue the life you were created for. You don't need a perfect background, the right degree, or a polished resume to be someone who makes an impact. You just need a vision, some grit, a whole lot of faith, and the willingness to show up day after day and do the work.

Maybe your version of success looks different than mine. That's okay. It should. But no matter what your dream is, it all starts with what you believe, what you repeat, and how you serve.

If you're going to build something, build it on faith. Build it with heart. Build it to last.

Your story is still being written, so go ahead—rewrite the stars!

CHAPTER THIRTEEN

Sarita Rodriguez
Recalibrate Wellness
Owner

www.recalibratewellness.com
https://linktr.ee/RecalibrateWellness?utm_source=linktree_admin_share

For 16 years, I thrived in the beauty industry as a stylist and makeup artist, running my own image consulting business and helping clients look and feel their best. While I loved transforming outer appearances, I realized that true confidence and wellness come from within. This realization inspired me to pivot my career and start Recalibrate Wellness, where I help others transform their health and lives from the inside out.

Now, as an Integrative Nutrition Health Coach, RYT 200, and Ayurvedic Specialist, I empower individuals to take charge of their health through diet, lifestyle, and mindfulness practices. Currently pursuing my RYT 500 certification, I combine modern science with ancient traditions to guide clients toward balanced, sustainable wellness.

My passion lies in educating on preventative healthcare and showing how simple, consistent changes can profoundly impact overall well-being. Through Recalibrate Wellness, I'm dedicated to helping others create a foundation for lasting health and vitality.

Confidence, Connection, and Closing: The Mindset Shift for Coaching Success

By Sarita Rodriguez

Building a successful coaching business requires more than just skills and certifications. It takes confidence, self-worth, and the ability to connect authentically with clients. Yet many coaches, especially women, struggle with asking for money, overcoming rejection fears, and aligning their energy with success. This chapter explores how to build a mindset that empowers you to thrive by focusing on confidence, connection, and authenticity.

Confidence: The Cornerstone of Success

Confidence is the foundation of your coaching success. Without it, even the most effective strategies will fall short. Confidence isn't about perfection or knowing everything—it's about trusting your ability to provide value and help your clients transform their lives.

Unfortunately, many coaches tie their confidence to external factors, such as certifications or years of experience. While these are important, they do not define your ability to succeed. True confidence comes from taking action and learning through experience.

If you struggle with self-doubt, start by reflecting on the results you've already helped others achieve. If you are just starting out and do not have any clients, offer to speak at a community center or library. Hosting a "coffee/tea workshop" with a small group is just one idea to help you gain experience. Celebrate those wins and remind yourself that growth comes through action. Confidence builds as you continue to show up, refine your skills, and deliver value to your clients.

The Fear of Rejection and Asking for Money

One of the biggest challenges for female coaches is asking for money. Many worry about rejection or fear coming across as pushy or "salesy." I've come across a coach in my alumni circle who felt the average asking price for her services was too high. Her business was not generating what she needed because she was pricing her services with her personal budget in mind. This mindset can lead to undervaluing your services or avoiding sales conversations altogether.

Reframe your thinking around money, instead of focusing on how expensive it is or the fear of rejection, view pricing as a reflection of the value you provide. When clients invest in your services, they are committing to their own growth and transformation. Asking for money isn't about you—it's about the results you deliver.

Practice stating your prices with confidence, and don't take a "no" personally. A client's decision not to invest is often about their readiness, not your worth.

Worthiness: Owning Your Value

Self-worth plays a critical role in building a successful coaching business. If you don't believe you're worthy of success, it will show in your energy, pricing, and interactions with clients. Clients can sense hesitation, insecurity, or fear, which can create a disconnect and hinder trust.

Understand that your worth is inherent—it doesn't need to be earned or proven. Start by identifying any limiting beliefs you have about money or success. Replace these beliefs with affirmations such as, "I am worthy of abundance" or "My expertise brings immense value to my clients."

When you fully own your worth, you create a magnetic energy that attracts aligned clients who see and appreciate your value.

Education Doesn't Equal Qualification

A common misconception among coaches is that they need more certifications or qualifications before they can work with clients. While ongoing education is valuable, it's not the sole measure of your ability to coach effectively.

Your personal experiences, perspective, and unique approach are just as important as formal credentials. Clients are drawn to authenticity, not a laundry list of accolades. Remember, no one else can replicate your unique combination of skills, personality, and passion. Embrace your individuality and trust that it qualifies you to make an impact.

Clients Can Sense Fear or a Sales Pitch

Energy speaks louder than words. If you approach potential clients from a place of fear, desperation, or insecurity, they will sense it. Whether you're anxious about making a sale or unsure about your offer, that energy creates resistance.

Instead, focus on serving rather than selling. Shift your mindset to one of curiosity and connection. Ask yourself, "How can I genuinely help this person, even if they don't become a client?" By prioritizing the client's needs over your agenda, you build trust and leave a positive impression.

People don't want to feel like they're being sold to—they want to feel seen, heard, and understood. When you focus on connection, the conversation becomes about whether you're the right fit to help them rather than a transactional sale.

Dressing for the Part

Your appearance communicates a lot about your brand, professionalism, and the type of clients you want to attract. While it might seem superficial, dressing for success can significantly impact how you're perceived and how you feel.

This doesn't mean adopting a one-size-fits-all style. Instead, align your appearance with your values and the niche you serve. For instance, if you coach corporate professionals, polished attire is appropriate. If your niche is health and wellness, opt for a clean and approachable style that reflects the industry.

When you look the part, you project confidence, and that confidence will resonate with your clients.

Connection Over Selling

Many coaches make the mistake of viewing potential clients as transactions rather than people. While it's important to qualify clients, the process should never feel like you're simply sorting through leads to close a sale.

Focus on building genuine connections. Take the time to understand a client's needs, challenges, and goals. Create a space where they feel safe to share their struggles. When you approach conversations with authenticity and empathy, clients will naturally feel drawn to work with you.

Remember, it's not about convincing someone to hire you—it's about determining whether you're the right fit for their needs. By prioritizing connection over selling, you build relationships that lead to long-term success.

Shifting Your Mindset for Success

Success begins with your mindset. Here are strategies to help you build the confidence, worthiness, and authenticity needed to thrive:

1. Practice Self-Reflection

Regularly check in with yourself to identify any fears, insecurities, or limiting beliefs. Journaling, meditation, or working with a mentor can help you process and reframe these thoughts.

2. Celebrate Your Wins

Acknowledge and celebrate every success, no matter how small. Each win reinforces your confidence and reminds you of the value you provide.

3. Focus on Value, Not Validation

Shift your focus from seeking external validation to delivering value. Trust that the right clients will see your worth and be willing to invest.

4. Set Boundaries

Not every client is the right fit, and that's okay. Saying no to misaligned opportunities creates space for clients who resonate with your expertise and values.

5. Invest in Yourself

Continue to grow personally and professionally. Whether it's through education, self-care, or working with your own coach, investing in yourself enhances your ability to serve others.

Bringing It All Together

Success as a coach isn't about having all the answers or the perfect sales pitch—it's about showing up authentically and confidently, connecting with others, and staying true to your mission.

When you embrace your unique gifts, own your worth, and approach clients from a place of service, you'll naturally attract the right people into your business. Your coaching business is an extension of who you are, and when you lead with confidence and connection, success becomes inevitable.

To Learn More About Me and my practice

CHAPTER FOURTEEN

Michelle Torres
Titan Enterprize
High Peaks Construction Business Owner & Real Estate Investor

https://linktr.ee/ut.realtormichelle

Michelle Torres is a business coach dedicated to empowering entrepreneurs and business leaders to turn their goals into measurable success. With expertise in diverse industries, including being a realtor, real estate investor, automotive, beauty, and creative financing, I provide clear, actionable strategies to help businesses thrive. My mission is to support women in building sustainable and profitable futures.

I have been a business owner for over 30 years.

Helping Women Become Successful Entrepreneurs

By Michelle Torres

You know, most successful women started by having a dream. They have built their own beliefs and possibilities, worked hard, and had burning desires; they inspired themselves through their own experiences and sacrifices. I found myself going through these experiences and feelings.

I started helping my Father with his business at a really young age, "15". By the time I turned 17, I found a job at a fast food place, and I worked there for about 5 months. I realized that I needed to be there to help my father with his business. I saw that I was making someone else's dreams come true and making them rich when, in reality, I needed to be there to help my own father make his dreams come true, as well as supporting "us," his family. I helped my father for many years, doing auto body work and office work for him. While I was still in high school, fast forward many years later, when I turned 24, I opened my own Auto body and detailing shop. That's when I realized I would never work for anyone again. I would be my own boss. (Boss Lady)! I now have many different businesses. I have two tire shops and a construction company. I am a Realtor and Real Estate Investor.

Many women hesitate to start their entrepreneurial journey due to fear—fear of failure, fear of judgment, and fear of the unknown. This hesitation is often rooted in societal expectations and self-doubt.

"You don't rise to the level of your goals. You fall to the standard of your systems." This perspective shift is crucial: entrepreneurship isn't about fearlessness but about creating systems that support you when fear inevitably arises. The path to entrepreneurship isn't about eliminating fear but learning to act despite it. By building systems, focusing on creating value, and surrounding yourself with support, you can transform fear from a barrier into a catalyst for growth.

Remember these four things.

1. Imposter syndrome: Questioning if you're qualified or knowledgeable enough.

2. Financial insecurity: Worrying about stable income and supporting yourself or your family.

3. Work-life balance concerns: Fearing you'll sacrifice your personal life for business.

4. Fear of public perception: Worrying about what others will think if you fail.

"I struggled for years, financially, mentally, physically, and being a single, married Mom. It was hard for me to socialize, educate myself, work, and rear my children, as well as having many health problems. I had seven major surgeries during a time when I was working to figure out my business. A mistake of building a life around your business rather than building a business around your desired life."Define what type of life you want... What does your day look like? What's important to you?

This common experience highlights that entrepreneurship is a learning curve for everyone, regardless of background. I had to learn that the tension between discipline and a significant mindset shift involves moving from scarcity thinking to abundance thinking. The solution isn't eliminating hustle but changing its source. When your drive comes from wanting to create value rather than fear of not having enough, your business decisions become more aligned with long-term success.

This "no fear zone" mindset allows you to take calculated risks without the paralyzing fear of failure. Most women often undervalue their expertise or hesitate to claim their accomplishments. Practice owning your knowledge and being comfortable saying "I don't know" when appropriate. "There is so much power in admitting you don't know what you don't know, but not from a place of weakness." This authenticity builds trust with clients and partners while strengthening your self-confidence. This technique helps maintain control of business interactions and builds trust in your decision-making abilities. Shift your focus from your own fears to how you can help others. I surrounded myself with mentors and peers who understood my journey. I even joined a community of like-minded entrepreneurs providing both practical advice and emotional support. As a real estate entrepreneur, I love the community of collaboration that Successful entrepreneurs rely on systems rather than willpower or motivation. Create morning and evening routines that regulate your emotions and set you up for productive days. "Your morning routine and your nightly routine are purely to regulate your emotions. Most of us go to bed stressed with anxiety... Remember, there are going to be days when you do not feel like doing anything. No work, No Play, Nothing at all. When I had these days, I had to remember I had children and a husband. And they wanted me to be there for them… I told them I needed to be alone for a while to find myself so that I could be there for them. Find out what works for you because we, as Moms, need to keep our sanity. So, if you can go to bed a little earlier and get quality sleep, establishing these boundaries helps prevent burnout and maintains your focus. Rather than waiting for perfect conditions, begin with small, consistent steps. Mindset provides fulfillment that transcends financial success.

Identify the skills most relevant to your business and invest time in mastering them. "I would say those are the systems that I'd implement... night routine, morning routine, and then are you studying every day to sharpen the saw?" Continuous learning builds confidence and competence simultaneously. I found myself hiring coaches to help me in all aspects of my life.

Many women hesitate to start businesses due to financial insecurity. Consider starting your business while maintaining other income sources, or explore partnerships that distribute financial risk. Remember that entrepreneurship doesn't always require significant upfront investment—many successful businesses start small and reinvest profits for growth.

1. Personal growth: Overcoming challenges builds resilience and confidence
2. Flexibility: Creating a business that accommodates your life priorities
3. Impact: Solving problems and creating value for others
4. Legacy: Building something that can outlast your direct involvement

Women often juggle multiple responsibilities, making time management crucial. I had to do this daily, Learning to use time blocking to ensure both business and personal priorities receive attention.

Remember that entrepreneurship is a journey, not a destination.

Take steps in having a Strategic Planning and Action:

Breaking goals into 30- 60- 90-day sprints for momentum.

Make a call to action and reevaluate the quarterly review checklist.

Time management strategies, weekly check-ins, and accountability partners, especially for busy women like entrepreneurs, Stay-at-home moms, or women who work a 9-to-5 job.

By using these strategic planning and actions, you will help manage your time more productively.

While financial independence is important, entrepreneurship offers women much more. "Is it so important to work on what you actually want? Why are you doing this? What do you want out of life? Because if you're not making yourself happy, like it's all for nothing, like getting a bigger house or getting a better car or, like, better clothes, that really is so superficial it doesn't do anything to our actual happiness. We only have one life to live, and how are you going to live it?

"Think very long term, always do the right thing... The difference between people who fail and people who succeed is that the ones who fail just give up. If you stay in the game long enough, even if it's difficult, even if you're struggling, even if it's not going well, if you stay in the game, you have a chance to win.

Your entrepreneurial journey begins with a single step. What will yours be? What will get you there?

I myself invested in making cash flow work for me. Cash flow VS profit Cash flow is the money that keeps your business afloat. What is going in is also going out in that everyday rotation.

Profit is the money you're making to be able to spend on your wants and needs. Basically, your leftover money after all the expenses are subtracted from your revenue.

Statistic: An increase in women-owned businesses happened during the COVID-19 pandemic and is still increasing. LETS GO WOMEN!

Questions?

Here's My linktree
Scan for Socials and Contact INFO
Let's stay in touch!

CHAPTER FIFTEEN

Sanya Bari, MEd, LPC, NCC

Relationship Trauma Therapist & Coach

Creator of the Love Clarity Method™

Host of the Love Clarity Podcast

Founder of the Love Clarity Inner Circle

Founder of the School for Transformational Healing

https://www.sanyabari.com/

Instagram: @Sanya.Bari

Sanya Bari helps people heal relationship trauma and love deeply without suffering—a method that she first used to save herself. A therapist and coach with over a decade of experience, she's guided Olympic athletes, federal judges, CEOs, and public figures through heartbreak, betrayal, narcissistic abuse, codependency, and divorce.

A survivor of relationship trauma, Sanya created the Love Clarity Method to help people identify the hidden patterns that keep them in trauma loops—unknowingly recreating the very pain they fear. Her framework introduces the Four Love Lies and teaches how to use emotional pain as a compass, not a curse.

Her clients learn to stop abandoning themselves and start creating love that feels free, safe, and rooted in their own center—regardless of anyone else's behavior.

Sanya blends clinical depth with soulfuLove Clarity Method: How to Love Deeply Without Losing Yourselfl clarity, making the emotional world simple, actionable, and transformative—so love becomes a source of peace, not pain.

Love Clarity Method: How to Love Deeply Without Losing Yourself

By Sanya Bari

At nine years old, sitting in the backseat on a family drive, I poked my head forward and declared:

"I'm going to fall in love, and I'm going to do it better than all of you. I'm going to figure out how to not get hurt in love."

My mother chuckled. My father smirked. Someone in the back muttered, "Love doesn't work that way."

But I didn't care. I was going to crack the code of love.

I wasn't interested in the quiet, functional love my parents shared—the kind that kept life running smoothly but lacked the spark I read about in stories. I wanted extraordinary love—love that felt limitless, love that couldn't be undone by issues or upsets.

At first, it was exciting—a puzzle to solve. Like a little scientist, I studied love, eavesdropping on adult conversations and watching the tension between words left unsaid. When my parents told me to "go play with the kids," I lingered—absorbing everything, searching for hidden clues to love.

But what started as fascination quickly turned into fear.

I saw relationships that had sparks and left people burned.

I watched my parents and wondered: Is love supposed to look like this?

Then I saw heartbreak hollow people out—and I adjusted.

Maybe love didn't need to be thrilling. Maybe I just needed safety. Reliability. Something that wouldn't hurt me.

Love merged into safety somehow, and control felt like the vehicle that would get me there. I made my life about controlling what I needed to avoid the pain. I curated myself into what I thought others would find lovable, acceptable, and valuable so I could be loved and, thus, safe.

I became a master of self-editing—a shape-shifter. I molded myself into whatever version of me might be most lovable, most acceptable, most... safe. I thought: if I played it safe, I'd be safe. If I chose love with my eyes open instead of falling blindly into it, I'd avoid getting hurt.

But fear dressed up as control is still fear. And fear only creates more of itself.

Everything I feared—betrayal, abandonment, neglect—kept playing on repeat. Through all stages of my life, from being a young child to a married mother of three, I experienced deep betrayals that cut at the same soft and sacred place I loved from.

As the pain grew, and fear of getting hurt grew, so did my control.

There's a Navajo saying: There are two wolves that live outside your door. One will eat you up and destroy you. The other will set you free. The one that grows is the one you feed the most.

Feed the fear, and the fear will grow. Feed the love, and the love will grow.

I fed the fear so much that it became my destruction.

At some point, the fear I was controlling started controlling me.

At some point, my armor became my prison, and I couldn't get out. I couldn't see how to stay in either. I was trapped in a never-ending loop of "If I do this, then that will happen." I became codependent and lost myself, demeaned myself in ways no betrayal from anyone else could match.

If I look like this, say this, study that... then maybe I'll be loved. I'll be safe. I'll be enough.

The harder it became to control things, the tighter I gripped—until one day, my suffering grew larger than the childhood hope I had been clinging to.

And when hope disappeared?

So did I.

I didn't plan on waking up.

But I did.

To a day I hadn't expected.

To a life I didn't know how to live.

To the stark, humiliating reality of being discovered—and my inability to even control my own death.

The plan was to disappear quietly. No note. No drama. Just an ending.

But waking up didn't feel like I'd been spared. It felt like I had nothing left to fight. And in that stillness, something changed.

I didn't come back with clarity—not at first. But something mysterious arrived with me. A strange new ability to witness my life from the outside. Not like my clinical training, where I could neutrally observe others, this was different. I didn't have to think about it. I could step outside myself and see what was happening without the filter of emotion.

And it was in that state of neutrality, while waiting to board a plane for a family vacation, that something clicked.

I saw—clearly, painfully—how often I hurt my kids, my husband, and the people I love, even while doing things I believed were loving.

The realization stung: I was often doing something loving from a place of fear.

That clarity hurt. And the questions I had carried all my life came rushing back.

How do I love deeply without suffering?

How do I love without losing myself?

Only this time, the answers started dropping in—like cue cards, one after another, as if they had a will of their own.

Before I could fully take in what was happening, the Four Love Lies arrived—each one carrying a sharp, clear truth about how we hurt others and ourselves when we think we're loving from a good place.

These truths became the foundation of the greater Love Clarity Method—a framework that helps you heal emotional mammoths like betrayal, narcissistic abuse, divorce, and codependency by creating a loving relationship with yourself—one that becomes the foundation of every other relationship in your life.

And maybe that little girl in the backseat wasn't wrong after all.

I did crack the code of love—not by avoiding the hurt, but by leaning into it, and learning how to stay whole in the face of it.

The Four Love Lies

These aren't just patterns. They're invisible contracts we sign with fear, mistaking them for love, even as they pull us away from it, and from who we truly are.

1. **Guilt**

Somehow, guilt became normalized as part of loving.

I'd say things like, "I felt so guilty I couldn't make it to your play, so let me take you out for lunch."

It sounded like love, but it wasn't. It was self-soothing disguised as generosity.

Like the time I showed up with cupcakes to school pickup after yelling at my child that morning, trying to buy back the love I feared I'd lost.

We proudly exchange guilt like battle scars.

I gave up everything for my kids.

I stayed even though it hurt.

Guilt tricks us into believing that love must hurt. But love doesn't ask for secret sacrifices—fear does.

Guilt sounds like: "I feel so bad. I should..."

2. Over-Responsibility

Doing for others what they can do for themselves.

It's widely praised. You're the "good mom," the "selfless partner," the "rock."

Like when I redid my teenager's project at midnight after working a full day—because I didn't want him to fail. He didn't ask me to. I just couldn't bear the discomfort of watching him stumble.

Over-responsibility feels like support, but it breaks the very person you're trying to help. It sends the message: You can't handle this. I'll do it.

Over time, you feel used. They feel controlled. And no one feels appreciated.

Over-responsibility sounds like: "I'll just take care of it."

3. Role-Playing

Not roles. **Role-playing.** Acting out what you think a "good partner" or "good parent" should be—even if it means abandoning what's real.

When I play the role of "Mom," I unconsciously force my child into the role of "Child."

When he steps outside the script I had in mind, I double down and push him back in.

We dehumanize each other this way—acting out old stories rather than writing new ones together.

And we do it in the name of love.

Role-playing sounds like: "I should... You should..."

4. Transactions

I used to think I didn't do transactions.

"I'm not keeping score," I'd say. "I'm doing this because I want to."

But every time I got hurt, it revealed an expectation I hadn't admitted to—even to myself.

Like when I listened patiently to everything my husband was going through, stayed up late supporting him, and told myself I didn't need anything in return.

But deep down, I was hoping he'd finally ask how I was doing.

When he didn't, I wasn't just disappointed—I felt invisible.

Not because of what he did, but because of what I had silently expected.

Transactions are often invisible.

If I love you enough, you won't leave.

If I help you succeed, you won't cheat.

If I give everything, you'll give it back.

But real love isn't a bargain. It's a gift.

The transaction sounds like: "If I do this, then you'll..."

Healing the Lies Without Reinforcing Them

Realizing these patterns can feel like a betrayal of everything you thought was good about you. But awareness doesn't have to bring shame—it can bring freedom.

That's why the Four Love Lies are not standalone insights—they are part of the **Love Clarity Method**, a method designed to help you heal without accidentally reinforcing what you're trying to dissolve.

Loving Deeply Without Losing Yourself

To love deeply without losing yourself, you must pause.

Check in.

Take **self-consent.**

And consciously lead with love.

Self-consent isn't just permission—it's awareness.

Without it, we unknowingly violate ourselves.

We give, stay, and sacrifice without ever asking: Do I want this? Is this love—or fear of losing it?

Like sexual consent, self-consent must be active, ongoing, and freely given—not driven by fear or assumed by habit.

With each pause, each moment of noticing a Love Lie, and each shift from fear to love, you begin to retrain your nervous system.

You move from a survival default that recreates suffering… to a thriving default that builds the life you actually want.

Love, in its purest form, is what remains when you stop trying to earn it, manage it, or bargain with it.

After recognizing the Four Love Lies, love becomes simpler—but not smaller.

It becomes clear, calm, centered, and connected.

It feels less like performing and more like being.

It looks like leaving the dishes for a moment because your child is laughing in the other room, and you want to catch them.

It looks like saying no without guilt, yes without fear, and asking yourself, before asking anyone else: Is this true for me?

It feels less like shrinking from the brightness within you, and more like claiming its glow, inviting others to shine more freely on their own.

It feels like breathing easier, because you're no longer carrying a relationship on your back.

That's the beginning of the love that nourishes and heals you.

And it starts with choosing, again and again, to love from the clarity of love, not fear.

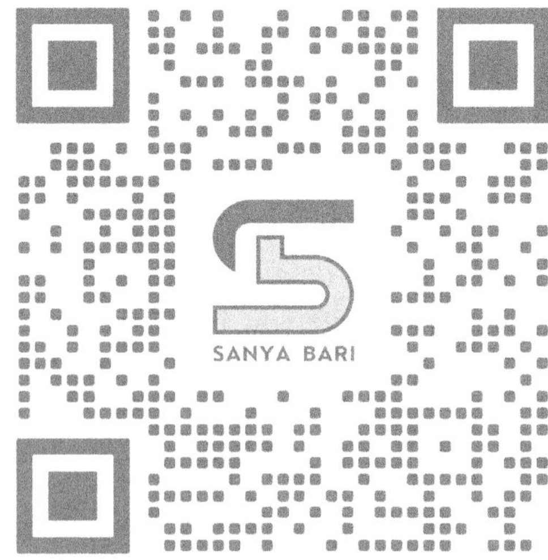

CHAPTER SIXTEEN

Jennifer Wright
Inspired Phoenix Enterprises, LLC
President

www.loansdonewright.org
htps://www.linkedin.com/company/inspiredphoenixenterprises/
https://www.instagram.com/jennifer_wright_mortgagebroker/
https://www.facebook.com/scorpiojenn

Jennifer is a multifaceted entrepreneur, humanitarian, and transformational leader with a passion for empowering others to rise, like a phoenix, into their greatness. As a life coach, board-certified clinical chaplain, best-selling author, and the visionary founder of her own mortgage brokerage and real estate investing company, Jennifer's work spans industries and inspires impact on both personal and professional levels.

Jennifer's extensive experience includes guiding clients through personal growth, navigating complex challenges, and helping them build their own empires with strength and clarity. Her humanitarian endeavors have fueled her commitment to serving communities, uplifting lives, and bridging divides across cultural and economic boundaries. Through her coaching, she provides individuals with the tools to reframe adversity, embrace transformation, and achieve their dreams.

Her leadership achievements include serving as past President of Valley West Rotary, Chairman of the Utah Brain Coalition, and Planning Commission Chairman. These roles reflect her dedication to fostering growth, collaboration, and meaningful change within her community. Whether mentoring future leaders or spearheading impactful initiatives, Jennifer's leadership exemplifies a commitment to service and vision.

Jennifer's dedication to lifelong learning, resilience, and servant leadership is at the heart of her success. Her unique approach draws from her diverse expertise, blending business acumen with empathy and authenticity. Whether leading humanitarian projects, mentoring future leaders, or building her thriving real estate ventures, Jennifer exemplifies what it means to create an empire built on purpose and perseverance.

Like A Phoenix Rising: Lessons from My Journey

By Jennifer Wright

Success is not born from a singular moment; it is a mosaic of experiences, challenges, triumphs, and lessons learned. My journey as a life coach, board-certified clinical chaplain, and humanitarian has been one of growth, purpose, and relentless dedication. Each step along this path shaped my perspective and cultivated my passion for guiding others to success. In this chapter, I aim to share insights that can empower and guide you on your own path to creating your empire, rising, like a phoenix, from adversity into greatness.

The Power of Authenticity

One of the first lessons I learned in my career was the importance of authenticity. Whether coaching a client, comforting a patient, or working within humanitarian efforts, people can sense when you are being genuine. Authenticity builds trust and fosters meaningful connections, enabling deeper and more impactful relationships.

Authenticity begins with self-awareness. It's about being honest with yourself and others, embracing your values, vulnerabilities, and unique voice. While there are moments of doubt and self-reflection, remaining true to who you are strengthens your ability to navigate uncertainty. It also creates a foundation for long-lasting and transformative connections with others.

- **Lesson Learned:** Be yourself unapologetically. Your values, voice, and vulnerabilities are the foundation of trust and influence.

- **Tip:** Practice self-reflection regularly to ensure your actions align with your true intentions and beliefs. Journaling or meditating on your core values can help reinforce this alignment.

Empathy as a Superpower

Empathy is the cornerstone of impactful coaching and leadership. It enables you to truly connect with others, fostering an environment of understanding and trust. As a chaplain, I witnessed how listening and validating someone's experience could profoundly impact their journey. In my humanitarian work, empathy became a tool to bridge divides and inspire solidarity across diverse communities.

Empathy is about presence and validation—it's not about rushing to solutions. This depth of connection creates the foundation for collaboration and growth, whether in coaching, leadership, or humanitarian outreach.

Lesson Learned: Empathy creates bridges where there may be divides. It allows you to see beyond surface issues and address the root of challenges.

Tip: Actively practice deep listening—don't just hear, but truly absorb what others are sharing. Respond with validation and understanding.

Resilience in the Face of Challenges

Like a phoenix rising from the ashes, resilience is the foundation of growth and renewal. My journey has been shaped by moments that tested my resolve. Challenges presented opportunities to learn and refine my approach, propelling me forward with greater strength and wisdom.

Resilience is cultivated by embracing adversity. Whether overcoming systemic challenges in humanitarian efforts or navigating personal setbacks, I've learned that resilience isn't just about bouncing back—it's about rising higher. These lessons helped shape my approach to empowering others through transformation.

- **Lesson Learned:** Challenges are stepping stones, not stumbling blocks. Resilience enables you to rise stronger and wiser.
- **Tip:** Develop a resilience toolkit—this may include mindfulness practices, supportive relationships, journaling, or physical movement to process emotions and maintain strength.

The Art of Communication

Effective communication is an essential skill in coaching, humanitarian work, and leadership. It's not just about expressing your thoughts but about fostering mutual understanding, building trust, and inspiring action.

Communication involves empathy, clarity, and adaptability. It is a skill that requires intention and continuous refinement. Whether guiding clients toward breakthroughs or navigating complex humanitarian situations, I have found that listening thoughtfully and responding purposefully are keys to creating solutions and sparking change.

- **Lesson Learned:** Communication is a two-way street. Conveying your thoughts while understanding others' perspectives is vital to success.
- **Tip:** Practice active listening and clarity in expression. Avoid overcomplicating language and use a tone that resonates with your audience.

Vision and Purpose

Creating an empire begins with a clear and compelling vision. Early in my career, I realized that purpose is like a lighthouse—it guides you through challenges and uncertainties, keeping you focused on what truly matters.

Vision provides clarity and motivation. My work has shown me the importance of anchoring your goals in purpose, ensuring that each step aligns with your mission. Whether leading humanitarian initiatives or empowering clients to define their path, I encourage vision-setting as the first step toward transformation.

- **Lesson Learned:** A strong sense of purpose keeps you motivated, even when obstacles arise.
- **Tip:** Write down your vision and revisit it often. Break it into actionable steps and let it serve as your guiding star.

Coaching Like a Phoenix Rising

My coaching style mirrors the phoenix—a symbol of transformation and renewal. I encourage clients to reframe challenges as opportunities to grow, rebuild, and rise stronger. Each setback is a chance to redefine your path with clarity and purpose.

The philosophy of the phoenix inspires resilience and optimism. It reminds us that adversity does not define us—it refines us. Through this lens, I've guided individuals to embrace change and rediscover their inner strength.

- **Lesson Learned:** Adversity is not an ending; it is a beginning. Transformation is possible when you embrace challenges with grace.
- **Tip:** Help clients channel their strengths and rise from challenges. Focus on the possibilities that arise from transformation.

Leadership through Service

True leadership is rooted in service. My humanitarian work showed me that service-driven leadership fosters collaboration, respect, and long-lasting impact. By prioritizing the needs of others, you create a culture of empowerment and shared success.

Leadership through service is about lifting others up and enabling them to realize their potential. Whether working with a client or leading a project, this approach creates ripples of positivity and change.

- **Lesson Learned:** Great leaders empower others to succeed. Leadership driven by service amplifies collective impact.
- **Tip:** Identify ways to support your community, team, or clients through mentorship, encouragement, or collaboration.

Balancing Ambition and Self-Care

Ambition fuels progress, but without balance, it can lead to burnout. At times, I've prioritized work above my well-being, learning the hard way that self-care is not optional—it is essential.

Self-care is the foundation of sustainability. It ensures you can maintain the energy and passion needed to pursue your goals while remaining present and grounded.

- **Lesson Learned:** Your empire is only as strong as its cornerstone: you. Self-care is vital to sustaining your energy and passion.
- **Tip:** Create rituals for rest and rejuvenation, whether through meditation, time in nature, or pursuing hobbies that bring joy.

The Power of Mentorship

Mentorship has been instrumental in my journey. Learning from experienced leaders and sharing insights with mentees has enriched both my personal and professional growth.

Mentorship is a partnership of mutual learning. It creates a cycle of empowerment, allowing wisdom to flow freely while forging meaningful connections.

- **Lesson Learned:** Seek mentors who inspire growth and be open to mentoring others—it's a cycle of learning and empowerment.
- **Tip:** Build meaningful relationships with mentors and mentees. Share your experiences and remain open to new perspectives.

Continuous Learning

Success is not a destination; it is a journey of lifelong growth. Staying curious and adaptable has allowed me to evolve and respond to challenges with creativity and confidence.

Continuous learning ensures relevance and resilience. Whether exploring new techniques, engaging with thought leaders, or tackling unfamiliar challenges, it has been central to my journey of self-discovery.

- **Lesson Learned:** Lifelong learning is essential for growth. Every experience is an opportunity to expand your knowledge.
- **Tip:** Seek out learning opportunities—attend workshops, read widely, and stay engaged with evolving practices.

Courage to Take Risks

Creating an empire requires boldness. Risks are stepping stones to progress, offering opportunities to grow beyond your comfort zone and achieve the extraordinary.

Taking risks has shaped my career, from launching my coaching business to leading humanitarian projects. Each leap of faith taught me the value of courage and the transformative power of embracing the unknown.

- **Lesson Learned:** Risk-taking is a necessary ingredient of success. Growth happens when you step outside your comfort zone.
- **Tip:** Approach risks with confidence and calculated planning. Learn from failures and use them as tools for growth.

Celebrating Successes

Celebrating milestones fosters motivation and gratitude. Whether it's achieving a personal goal or witnessing progress within a community, these moments deserve recognition.

Celebration reinforces positive behavior and reminds you of how far you've come. It creates an atmosphere of encouragement and fuels the drive to continue.

- **Lesson Learned:** Celebrate successes—big or small. Acknowledging achievements inspires further progress.
- **Tip:** Establish traditions for celebration—express gratitude, share your joy, and honor milestones meaningfully.

Final Thoughts

Creating your empire is about embracing the journey—its highs, lows, lessons, and triumphs. It's about knowing who you are, what you stand for, and the legacy you aim to leave behind. The path to success is neither linear nor easy, but it is profoundly rewarding. And remember, like a phoenix rising, every challenge you face is an opportunity to transform, renew, and ascend stronger than ever before.

CHAPTER SEVENTEEN

Alinda Rowley-Jensen
ARJ Investing
CEO

www.arjinvesting.com
https://www.instagram.com/arj_investing/
https://www.facebook.com/ARJInvesting
https://www.tiktok.com/@arjinvesting

Alinda Rowley-Jensen is the visionary founder of ARJ Investing, a company that has made a significant impact on the Utah real estate market. With a passion for helping others, Alinda has dedicated her career to assisting hundreds of Utah families in avoiding foreclosure and finding financial stability. Her deep understanding of real estate and commitment to community welfare have made her a trusted figure in the industry. Under Alinda's leadership, ARJ Investing has not only supported homeowners but also enabled investors to find real, profitable properties. Her innovative approach allows investors to take over existing mortgages, providing them with unique opportunities to expand their portfolios. This strategy has proven to be a game-changer, offering both investors and homeowners a path to success. Her work has not only transformed ARJ Investing into a thriving business but has also enriched the communities she serves.

Breaking Free: Three Steps to Transform Your Life Into An Abundant Future

By Alinda Rowley-Jensen

Building a business is never easy, and let me be clear: the path to your dreams isn't paved with roses. It is rough at times, a mixture of sharp edges and velvet moments, highs of dazzling gold and lows that feel like deep, cold waters. But the hardest thing of all—the real pain—is never daring to try.

It took me more than half of my life to realize I was worthy of investing in myself. Imagine living half your life in muted shades of gray, afraid to dream in vibrant hues. However, the second half of my life bursts daily with colors of possibility, filled with radiant abundance and lush opportunities that taste sweet, sound like laughter, and feel like warm sunlight.

Nothing worth having is ever simple. Even when it seems straightforward, the reality is layered, complex, and deeply personal. Every interaction, every exchange is a negotiation. I think back to conversations with my teenagers — every interaction was an emotional dance, intricate and delicate. It was a game, and the strongest commitment to the result would ultimately win. I think of my ex-husband (and thank God he's my ex); our marriage was a constant tug-of-war in my mind, working through the insults and lack of support, telling myself deep inside I must "NOT" be worthy because he said so. Of course, this was not true, but it took all of my courage to convince myself. Now, above all, the most significant negotiation was always within myself.

Let me share this clearly and vividly, as I break down this journey into three simple steps. You're not crazy, you're not alone, and if I found my way, so will you. Remember, I chose PINK as my color, a passionate, feminine reminder of who I wanted—and deserved—to become. These steps are simplified so you will get the point quickly and take action immediately.

Step One: How to Win the Daily Negotiation with Yourself

The first step is deceptively simple yet profoundly challenging: every day, wake up and negotiate your way out of that comfort zone. Imagine your comfort zone as a cozy but suffocating blanket—soft, familiar, but keeping you trapped. Each morning, look in the mirror and remind yourself that you deserve more than comfort—you deserve extraordinary. Speak to your reflection like your best friend, wearing confidence like your favorite lipstick shade, and boldly declare, "I own my past, my present, and my future."

At ARJ Investing, our goal sounds straightforward: help homeowners facing foreclosure find a lifeline. But like the perfect pair of heels that pinch just a bit too tight, the reality is never as comfortable as we imagine. When I first started, I naively thought people would welcome us with open arms—after all, we offered a lifeline when the waters were rising fast.

Instead, my team and I often sift through dozens of conversations—sometimes 50 or more—to find one brave soul willing to accept help. Why? Accepting help means stepping into vulnerability, shedding layers of pride that sometimes feel as protective as armor. I've come to understand this deeply: often, we become our own harshest critics, fiercely resistant, even when help arrives wrapped in kindness.

Here's the bright-pink truth: It's far easier to talk ourselves into financial ruin or emotional quicksand than to reach out and grab hold of change.

And though I still wonder why we chose this painful path, I've learned we can rewrite our stories. It takes work, daily effort, and the steady courage found in small victories. So, remind yourself daily—inaction carries more heartache than any temporary stumble toward greatness.

Step Two: Eliminate Judgment

The second step demands you toss out judgment, like old clothes you've outgrown; it no longer serves you. Let's face it, judgment is exhausting. It colors your world in dull grays and bitter hues, whispering doubts, weighing you down with invisible burdens. Instead, consciously choose words that uplift, empower, and inspire—words that feel like silk against your skin, softening your outlook and brightening your days.

Learning to accept your reality without judgment is a skill, and it takes practice. Imagine clearly seeing yourself exactly where you are—not drowning, but swimming, strong and graceful, cutting through life's waves with courage and clarity. Recognizing your situation without shame or blame grants you true power, the strength of authenticity.

Acceptance is not about surrender; it's about bravely facing your truth, like looking directly into the sunlight until your vision adjusts and clarity emerges. When you can openly acknowledge your struggles without pity or criticism, you transform those struggles into stepping stones.

Every moment of successful transformation I've witnessed began from a place of clear-eyed acceptance. You simply cannot fix what you refuse to face. Embrace your truth without judgment, and allow it to ignite a fierce determination within you—a determination beautifully, unforgettably wrapped in your unique shade of PINK.

Step Three: Consistent Action Will Set You Free

The final step is all about consistent action—your golden thread that weaves dreams into reality. Imagine your daily actions as brush strokes on a canvas: each small, deliberate movement contributes to a breathtaking masterpiece. Life and business, just like art, thrive on resilience, flexibility, and daily commitment.

Begin by forming simple, beautiful habits—small routines that add sparkle and structure to your day. Evaluate your progress often, reflecting gently, adjusting thoughtfully. Did something work wonderfully? Lean into it. Did something fall short? Adapt with grace and determination, without pausing for discouragement.

When we founded ARJ, I committed to daily door-knocking, daily phone calls—each step grinding yet strangely empowering. Every conversation, every note captured, every adjustment made was a stroke of intention, clarity, and strength.

I deeply understand that feeling of struggle before achieving consistent success. But remember, every action taken moves you closer—even when results seem hidden. Celebrate the small, glorious victories, learn tenderly from setbacks, and never let anything interrupt the momentum of your beautiful journey.

The Future You Picture is Waiting for You

My friends, your abundant, vibrant future isn't a distant dream—it's right here, waiting for you to simply color in the lines. At ARJ, investing in ourselves and others has created profound joy and tangible success. We've saved over 200 families from foreclosure, safeguarded more than $110 million in residential real estate, keeping communities vibrant and hopeful.

Your journey toward success begins the moment you reach out. Don't wait another day— let's start coloring your future with brilliant possibilities. Trust me, you'll be fabulous.

CHAPTER EIGHTEEN

Shay Stone
PopRock Fitness and Nutrition/PopRock Realty
Owner, Certified Nutritionist and Personal Trainer/ Real Estate

www.poprockfitness.com
https://linktr.ee/shaystonewithpoprock
https://www.facebook.com/shay.m.stone
www.linkedin.com/in/shay-stone-770073307

Shay Stone has built her Estate Empire in the Mountains of Utah. She has created four businesses as a single mother raising two incredible boys. After her own hard life struggles, her journey of self-discovery has helped hundreds of people on their paths. She is a Certified Nutritionist, Personal Trainer, and Yoga Instructor and has worked for decades with athletes of all ages to help them rediscover themselves and reconnect with their bodies. In 2020, her expertise in finance shifted her path into the world of Real Estate. Her self-conquering attitude and ambition for life are contagious as she trains others to break their physical boundaries. This same passion has helped her transcend successfully through multiple business industries. She currently owns and operates a youth fitness gym in Lehi, Utah.

I would love to help anyone who may connect with my story in food, health, or Real Estate. Reach out. Text, email, or call me. Let me help you rediscover yourself.

You Can

By Shay Stone

I was a lost soul until I was thirty.

After that, I learned that I wasn't lost; I just wandered my own way. I pave my own path through thistles and thorns, but people don't realize it is also where you see the untouched beauty of the world. The wildflowers are for the wild ones. I am that girl. Curiosity pulls at me deeply. As a child, I learned that when someone told me no, it just meant to find it myself or do it my own way. I won't let anyone tell me what I can and cannot do.

I grew up in the High Uintah Mountains, thirty miles away from the closest grocery store or high school. My parents are devout Latter-day Saints or Mormons, which was the only building in town. As a family, we worked a 1,500-acre farm, along with milking 500 head of cattle twice daily. We also had every kind of animal you could hardly think of in the Northern US. We learned deeply the meaning of hard work and that the day starts long before the sun comes up.

When I was 16, my father lost everything. He didn't declare bankruptcy but instead gave everything up to pay his creditors. For that, I will respect him until the day I die. To honor your word. It matters. Who you are is built by your honor.

After I went to college, I packed on the freshman 15; mine was 30. I never felt more out of place than in a conventional gym. Walking on a treadmill or a stair stepper was monotonous. The mirrors made me uncomfortable, and the wandering eyes from men didn't help. Farm life and real life were very different things.

So, instead of finding myself or my body, I got married and had two babies.

I was 28 and miserable. I can't say I had lost myself because I never knew who I ever was, to begin with. Growing up Mormon, you are taught to be a certain way. Meek, humble, kind, obedient. One should strive for perfection. All the things I wasn't. I lived with the guilt of being anything but perfect. I hated my marriage, and I had two small boys I tied up in the mess. I didn't believe in the religion, but leaving meant being ostracized from my family and community completely. Truly being alone. I was the first person to leave our family since the pioneers had walked the plains. The guilt turned into weight as I ate my feelings each night before bed. I had accepted my unhappy fate. Like everyone in my family, I was heavy and would die that way.

Later that week, the doctors told me I had a tumor in my brain. Growing old and dying fat was not going to be an option for me. I instantly knew I wanted to live whatever life I had left the happiest, healthiest way I could. That meant change. Real change came with the acceptance of where I was in my life. Taking care of my body and my health wasn't something anyone else could do for me. No one was standing next to me to slap the junk food out of my hands before I shoveled it in my face. If I wanted this, it was on me to do it. This is when I learned what accountability to myself and what self-care truly mean.

I was 5'6" and over 200 pounds. This wasn't going to be easy, but I wanted to conquer myself, my bad habits, and my eating disorder issues. Acknowledging what I didn't know was the first step. I had to own up to the fact that I didn't know how to do the most basic thing, how to eat.

When I learned how to train my body for who I wanted to be instead of who I was told I should be, everything changed.

This time was going to be different, which meant I had to be different, which meant starting off small. Baby steps.

I focused on moving. It seemed less daunting and fun to do. I was too embarrassed to go to a gym, so this time I hired a coach. I fell in love with lifting and found functional fitness/CrossFit, which mimicked farm life. I learned that it doesn't matter what workout you do, as much as the happiness it brings. That the community of the gym matters as much as the workouts. Lifting heavy teaches you how to push hard in and outside the gym walls. When you really want something, with patience and practice, you can achieve it. Progress comes in small increments and over time. The closer you get to the goal, the harder it will become. Press deep into the ground and find your grit when things get tough. Breathe when things are heavy. Don't stop pushing.

Change does happen overnight. After you rest. It is in the act of sleeping and recovering that our muscles rebuild, grow, and we become stronger. The gym is where we rip them apart, not where we get stronger; that is in our beds with restful sleep. Sleep matters. Dreams only come after you lay in your bed and daydream. Without our dreams, we can't discover who we want to become.

I hit a 25-pound plateau. If movement brings life, comfort brings death. The gym had become routine. Now my challenge was my food. Clean up your nutrition, and you clean up your life. I hired another coach. I also fell in love with my body. I also fell in love with myself.

I didn't know my body could have a thigh gap.

I didn't know I had muscles, abs, a killer body under all of that fat.

I didn't know I would have so much energy.

I didn't know if my skin would clear up or if my cramps would go away.

I didn't know I could have a better body at 33 than at 23, and after babies.

I didn't know my body could ever crave vegetables and hate Doritos.

I didn't know the reason I couldn't do a pull-up was because of my extra 5 pounds.

I didn't know my sex drive would go through the roof.

I didn't know that I could walk on my hands, or run a marathon or do a triathlon.

I didn't know eating clean would give me a clearer mind for my business.

That my whole life would change, because of food… Real Food.

Food heals the body from the inside out, and in turn, it heals the soul. It is medicine.

After that, I went back to school and became a Registered Dietitian, personal trainer, Level 2 CrossFit Coach, and yoga instructor. I now own and operate a youth gym in hopes of giving them a place to find themselves through developing bodies and movement in life. I have almost two decades of experience helping hundreds of clients, from moms and dads to teens, children, and the elderly since that time. I have worked with amputees, diabetics, autoimmune issues, fertility issues, Games Athletes, and people from around the world.

It doesn't matter what size, age, or shape they are in; these are our principles:

1. Start the day early; you will always beat everyone else out before they even wake up.

2. Honor your word. Not only to others but to yourself. The promises you make to yourself matter.

3. Work hard means hard work. It won't be easy. Nothing is worth value.

4. Don't give up on yourself or what you want. You will pay with misery if you don't.

5. Be true to yourself. Don't let anyone tell you who and how to be the best version of you.

6. Life is short. Act and live like it matters.

7. If you want to change, the only person who can do it is you.

8. Don't give up, even if you have failed over and over again. Take a piece of knowledge from it, and then it isn't a failure.

9. Take ownership and accountability for yourself, what you say, and what you do.

10. Ask for help when needed. Accepting that we don't know is the hardest step there is. Asking for help is the second.

11 Start off small. One glass of water, one vegetable, one squat. You are never too old to become better. That is why you were given another day.

12. Movement is life. Train your body for who you want to become.

13. Sleep matters! Your dream life only comes if you dream.

14. Food heals. - You will not understand this if you do not earn it.

15. Go for things you never thought possible. You will become better than you ever can imagine.

Thinking

By Walter D. Wintle

If you think you are beaten, you are;

If you think you dare not, you don't.

If you'd like to win, but you think you can't,

It is almost certain you won't.

If you think you'll lose, you've lost;

For out in this world, we find,

Success begins with a fellow's will

It's all in the state of mind.

If you think you're outclassed, you are; You've got to think high to rise, and You've got to be sure of yourself before You can ever win the prize.

Life's battles don't always go

To the stronger or faster man,

But sooner or later the man who wins is the man who thinks he can!

CHAPTER NINETEEN

Maralana Shindelbower
Maralana Go Do Be
Owner

Maralana.com
http://linkedin.com/in/maralanagodobe
Instagram.com/MaralanaGoDoBe
Facebook.com/MaralanaGoDoBe

Maralana is a powerhouse of authenticity, boldness, and heart. Since 2012, she's coached women through life's biggest transitions, helping them break free from burnout, reconnect with themselves, and live unapologetically empowered lives.

She's the founder and Motivational Trainer of Go Do Be Empowered Life and the creative force behind journals, workbooks, and the TV show Big Girl Adventure Life, inspiring plus-size women to step into outdoor adventures and self-love.

As an author and speaker, Maralana blends storytelling, strategy, and real talk into everything she does. Her upcoming book delivers her signature mix of humor, truth, and action steps—designed to help you embrace your quirks, rediscover your confidence, and show up boldly.

She's not just talking about transformation...she is the transformation. And now she's here to help you Go. Do. Be. the fullest, fiercest version of YOU.

The Power of Owning All of You – Why Your Success Lies in Your Multifaceted Self

By Maralana Shindelbower

Do you know what I love more than a woman who's got her life perfectly together?

A woman who knows she doesn't have to.

We live in a world that keeps telling us to niche down, tone it down, calm it down, stay in our lane, and, for the love of branding, pick one thing. But here's what I want to tell you: You are not too much, you are many things. And that? That's your superpower.

Welcome to your next level, my friend, the one where you stop fighting who you are and start using it.

You're The Multifaceted Woman: Not a Mess, a Masterpiece

If you're anything like me (and if you're reading this, you probably are), you've felt the pressure to simplify yourself. Maybe you've been told to "just focus" or to stop being so "all over the place." You might have even tried to pick one path, just one neat little box to live in, but it never felt right, did it?

Because you weren't designed to be one-dimensional.

You are a mother, a creator, a strategist, a CEO, a nurturer, a wild dreamer, a spreadsheet queen, a Sunday napper, a TikTok scroller, and an early riser. You are all that and more, and trying to hide or shrink any of it to "fit the mold" is the fastest way to burn out and lose your fire.

Multifaceted women succeed not despite their many parts but because of them.

When you embrace your multifaceted magic, you unlock what I call aligned ambition, where your goals don't just look good on paper; they feel good in your bones. That's when success doesn't just show up in your business; it shows up in your joy, your confidence, your peace, and your purpose.

So no, you don't have to choose between being professional and passionate, polished and playful, ambitious and authentic. You get to be all of it and lead from the fullness of who you are.

Authenticity Isn't a Buzzword, It's the Bridge

Once you've acknowledged that you're a multifaceted powerhouse (and you are), the next challenge is knowing how to actually show up that way in your life, work, or business.

And this is where authenticity comes in, not as a trendy concept, but as the bridge between who you are and how you lead.

Because here's the thing: owning your many layers doesn't mean showing all of them at once or performing them for approval. It means being aligned. It means your values, your voice, and your visibility match. No more shape-shifting to fit in. No more hustling to be palatable or polished.

Authenticity is what allows your multifaceted identity to have an impact.

It's about saying:

"This is what I believe in. This is how I operate. This is what matters to me, and if it's not for you, that's fine. But I'm done editing myself for the illusion of acceptance."

Let me give it to you straight. So many women have been taught to be professional first, and personal second, or to fit a mold before they follow a mission. But authenticity flips that. It says, bring all of you to the table. Your quirks. Your instincts. Your voice. Your leadership. That's where your true power lies.

Because, let's be honest, people aren't craving more perfection. They're craving connection. And they connect with what's real.

You don't need to "find your voice; you just need to stop muting it.

When you do that, when you lead and build from the truth of who you are, you naturally become more magnetic. Not because you're louder or shinier, but because you're finally resonant. You're no longer broadcasting from someone else's frequency. You're tuned into your own.

And that's when we talk about passion.

Passion Isn't Optional, It's Your Engine

So if Authenticity gives you the permission to be all of you, then Passion gives you the fuel to do something powerful with it. It's essentially your engine.

You can know who you are, you can be aligned with your truth, but without passion, you're running on autopilot. Passion is the pulse that turns ideas into movement. It's the spark that keeps you going when you're tired, frustrated, or stuck in the messy middle.

And no, passion isn't just about what feels good. It's about what feels right, what you can't ignore. What stirs something in you? What you'd talk about, build around, or fight for even if no one clapped.

It's not fluffy. It's foundational.

Because let's be real, this work we're doing, whether it's coaching, leading, creating, building, or serving, it is hard sometimes. There are setbacks, doubts, quiet launches, and messy pivots. But when you're rooted in passion, you keep showing up. Not because it's easy, but because it matters.

So, when you feel disconnected, lost, or uninspired, don't try to hustle your way out of it. Reconnect to your passion. Ask yourself:

- What am I doing that lights me up?
- What feels heavy because it's out of alignment?
- What keeps calling me back, even when I've tried to walk away?

Because passion isn't always loud, sometimes it's a whisper that says, This is worth it.

Practical Tools to Unleash Your Multifaceted, Authentic, Passion-Fueled Self

Alright, now let's get into the good stuff, the how, because all the inspiration in the world means nothing if we don't turn it into action.

1. Create Your Facet Inventory

Grab a notebook (or open that Notes app, I see you, digital queen). Write down every part of who you are that lights you up. Think about passions, skills, interests, and identities. Don't edit. Don't judge.

- What do people come to you for?
- What brings you joy even when no one's watching?
- What parts of yourself have you been hiding or minimizing?

This list is gold. These are your tools, your content, your connections, your edge. Use them.

2. Build Your Core Values Roadmap

Success without values is empty. Take time to define what you stand for.

Choose 3–5 core values that feel deeply aligned to you (not what you should choose, but what actually resonates). Then, ask yourself:

- Is my business or work reflecting these?
- Do my daily choices support these values?
- Where am I out of alignment?

When your values and your vision match, everything flows more easily.

3. Turn Passion into Purpose

Pick one thing you're wildly passionate about. Now ask:

- How can I turn this into a message?
- How can this become a movement?
- How can this solve a problem?

Hint: Passion + Problem = Purpose. That's how you create offers, content, careers, or businesses that actually make an impact and income.

4. Start Before You're Ready, Show Up While You're Messy

Please don't wait until your ducks are in a row. Half of mine are still drunk in the parking lot.

Start now with what you've got from where you are. Your clarity will grow as you move.

Remember, people don't connect with perfection. They connect with the real. So be real. Be bold. Be in progress. That's where the magic lives.

I want to leave you with this:

You are not too much. You are not behind. You are not confused.

You are exactly where you're meant to be. And you're ready.

Success isn't reserved for the women with the most polished feeds, perfect routines, or rigid 10-year plans. It's reserved for the women who show up, own their magic, and stay in the game.

So say it with me:

- I don't have to pick one part of myself. I honor all of me.
- I don't have to follow the formula. I am the formula.
- I don't need permission. I give it to myself.

Because the moment you step fully into your multifaceted, authentic, passionate self?

That's the moment you become unshakable.

Now go out there and Go. Do. Be. all that you are.

Your people are waiting.

Your purpose is waiting.

And success is waiting, too!

CHAPTER TWENTY

Dr. Vicki Coleman
The Coleman Group
President/CEO

www.angerdr.com
www.Instagram.com/AngerDoctor
www.Facebook.com/DrVickiDColeman
www.TikTok.com/@DoccoleAnger www.Twitter.com/DrVicki

Dr. Vicki D. Coleman is an Internationally Recognized Behavioral Health Specialist, Psychologist, Best Selling Author, Professor, Researcher, and Talk Show Host.

A former Tenured Professor at Purdue University in West Lafayette, IN, she has also held positions at the State University of New York and American Airlines. As a researcher, she has several refereed publications on counseling strategies, sports psychology, career development, and multicultural populations.

As President/CEO of The Coleman Group & The Anger Doctor, she globally consults for education, business, industry, government, and professional associations.

A native of Detroit, Michigan, Dr. Coleman earned Bachelor's and Master's degrees from The University of Iowa; a Master's from Northern Illinois University; and a Doctorate in Counseling Psychology from Rutgers University in New Brunswick, NJ.

As a Sports Psychologist working with student, professional, and retired athletes, she is also completing her sports certification as a Transformation Specialist and Personal Trainer from the International Sports Sciences Association (ISSA).

Dr. Vicki D. Coleman is represented by Bruce Merrin, of the Bruce Merrin Celebrity Speakers & Entertainment Bureau, www.brucemerrinscelebrityspeakers.com.

Everyday Woman's Guide to Success

By Dr. Vicki Coleman

Success is a very personal definition! It is critical and especially important that individuals determine their definition and perception of this word and process, especially women in the 21st-century global economy.

With the complexities of the lifestyles of many women who strive for work-life balance, success is a concept that must be addressed.

SELF-CONCEPT AND SELF-ESTEEM

The initial step in striving for success is to know yourself with respect to Self-Concept and Self-Esteem.

Self-concept is the perception of what we think of ourselves, and Self-Esteem is how we feel about ourselves. These are critical components of success for women.

When discussing success, consider the six (6) Areas of Self-Concept and Self-Esteem that I modified from the research of Fitts & Warren (1964 & 1996).

- Personal Self-Concept and Self-Esteem

  Values, core beliefs, world view

- Physical Self-Concept and Self-Esteem

  Physical, physiological, and body image

- Family Self-Concept and Self-Esteem

  Biological family of origin, others identified as family.

- Social/Community Self-Concept

  Friends, neighbors, city, county, state, and country, global relationships

- Academic/Work/Professional/Financial Self-Concept and Self-Esteem

  Education, colleagues, professional, and financial endeavors

- Moral/Ethical/Spiritual Self-Concept and Self-Esteem (Coleman, 2008, 1992)

  Ethical, legal, spiritual considerations, why are we here, the reason for being

There are a variety of interventions and activities that will assist women in the self-assessment and self-discovery process related to Self-Concept and Self-Esteem. For example, identifying a professional behavioral health individual, such as a psychologist or therapist, is a focus.

Coleman, Success, cont'd.

Emotional regulation, journaling, and participating in networking and support groups for women, to name a few.

Understanding the Self in each of the above 6 Areas of Self-Concept and Self-Esteem is a critical step in facilitating success for women.

TRAUMA

Personally, I strongly believe that all individuals have suffered from trauma, and it is critical to identify any trauma sustained during early childhood and/or adolescence, including the implications and repercussions of said trauma on current thinking, decision-making, and behavior, among others.

Oftentimes, due to a variety of factors, such as culture, ethnic identity, family background, socialization, politicization, economic factors, and attitudes toward mental health interventions, trauma may not have been addressed during the early childhood and adolescent life stages.

If trauma is not appropriately identified, addressed, and understood, including interventions. It may lead to serious implications and repercussions during adulthood, with a major influence on thinking, decision-making, and behavior, including success in personal, couple, family, career, and financial endeavors, to name a few.

Healing from the trauma will have a positive effect on personal and professional growth and development. Cognitive Behavior Therapy (CBT), Rational Emotive Behavior Therapy (REBT), and Dialectical Behavior Therapy (DBT) are evidence-based therapeutic approaches that I utilize quite frequently when addressing clients' and patients' traumatic experiences.

CBT, REBT, and DBT address irrational belief systems, thinking errors, emotional regulation, mindfulness, and Self-Concept and Self-Esteem, among others.

DECISION MAKING

How do you make decisions? What are your decision-making strategies and styles? The major question is, "Are the strategies and styles I utilize affording me the ability and opportunity to make positive, satisfying, and appropriate decisions?"

CAREER DEVELOPMENT/MENTORS/NETWORKING/ TECHNOLOGY

In my Model of Career Development (Coleman, 2008; 1992), I indicate that career development is life development, an ongoing process of lifelong education and learning.

Coleman, Success, cont'd.

The Model includes a discussion of identifying values, core beliefs, strengths, skills, talents, and areas of improvement, to name a few. Educational, occupational, and community information, including preparation for work, leisure, and retirement, is also considered when dealing with one's career development.

Two (2) excellent strategies for facilitating the success of women are identifying mentors who can serve as role models and networking with women and men who can offer assistance, guidance, support, and referrals related to our career development aspirations.

These individuals and groups are located in every community, and with technology, we are oftentimes able to identify mentors and groups on an international or global level.

Resources such as colleges, universities, businesses, industry, government, not-for-profit organizations, and professional and learned associations offer a wealth of information and resources to inform and facilitate the process for women to succeed.

In the 21st century global economy, emerging developments and advances in technology offer a new and exciting experience for being successful in family, work, and life.

BARRIERS AND OBSTACLES

Barriers are obstacles that prevent us from getting what we want, doing what we want, and achieving our goals, among others (Coleman, in

Ventura-Rozen & Giles, 2021; Coleman, in Weighman, 2023; Coleman & Barker, 1992, 1991).

Barriers and Obstacles can be Internal or External:

Internal Barriers or Obstacles are those within us that are easier to identify and control, such as low self-concept, self-esteem, or fear.

External Barriers or Obstacles are those outside of us that are not easy to identify and control (if ever) and related to the environment, including the global economy.

Internal Barriers or Obstacles:

- Lack of Confidence
- Frustration, Fear, Anxiety, or Mental Disorder
- Low Self-Concept and/or Low Self-Esteem
- Lack of Specific Skills, Abilities
- Lack of Understanding of Relationships between Individuals, Groups, & Society
- Cultural Expectations

Coleman, Success, cont'd.

What are the implications of Internal Barriers on the success of women?

External Barriers or Obstacles:

- Global Economy
- Lack of Opportunity
- Health Care Availability & Limitations

- Stereotypes & Discrimination
- Local Economy & Environment
- Cultural Implications

What are the implications of External Barriers on the success of women?

SHORT/LONG-TERM GOALS

To facilitate success, consider utilizing the SMART Approach to add meaning and context to your short- and long-term goals.

The SMART Approach to goal setting is an extremely popular strategy and technique for establishing short- and long-term goals.

Originally developed by Management Consultant George T. Doran in 1981, the SMART Goal approach is listed below:

S – Specific

M – Measurable

A – Achievable

R - Relevant

T – Time Bound

This goal-setting paradigm allows one to establish short- and long-term goals that advance beyond a wish or idea, with a very specific purpose, timetable, and plan.

On a regular basis, I utilize the SMART Approach as a guide to ensure that my goals are congruent with my values, core beliefs, and world view and to also increase the probability of actually realizing the plans that I established.

When utilizing the SMART Approach, consider initially establishing goals for one (1) year, then five (5) years, and ten (10) years and beyond.

Coleman, Success, cont'd.

SELF-CARE

Finally, I believe that for women to be successful, we must attend to our Self-Care needs on a regular basis.

Self-care is identifying and implementing strategies and techniques that result in us feeling better about ourselves, including fun, rest, and relaxation.

Self-care is an individual endeavor with no right or wrong template. Self-care can be strategies, techniques, skills, and resources that prevent burnout.

Burnout, which can occur in all professions (Leiter & Schaufeli, 1996), is a work-related stress syndrome resulting from chronic exposure to job stress. The term, introduced in the early 1970s by psychoanalyst Freudenberger and subsequently defined by Maslach et al., consists of three qualitative dimensions, which are 1) emotional exhaustion; 2) cynicism and depersonalization; and 3) reduced professional efficacy and personal accomplishment (Freudenberger, 1975, 1977; Maslach, Schaufeli, & Leiter, 2001; &. Maslach & Jackson, 1981). (Coleman, VD. (2023). Dare to Care: Focus on Self-Care, 1st. In Weihman, M.R.).

The major goal of Self-Care is to prevent burnout, which is a psychological syndrome that can affect career success, with serious implications and repercussions.

So, what is your Self-Care Plan?

REVIEW OF STEPS/PROCESS

We must conduct a comprehensive review of the steps and processes that might facilitate success for women. Reviewing the steps and process will ensure that we have adhered to a specific plan of action, and identified any implications and repercussions that might need to be considered.

A comprehensive review of the steps and process will afford the opportunity to make changes and corrections, and include additional information as women continue to forge ahead with personal, couple, family, financial, and professional endeavors.

Coleman, Success, cont'd.

References

Coleman, V.D. (2008, 1992). Six Areas of Self-Concept & Self-Esteem. *Unpublished Manuscript.*

Coleman, V.D. (2008). A model of career development: 21st century applications. *Australian Career Practitioner*, *Spring*, *19,* 19-20.

Coleman, V.D. & Barker, S.A. (1992). A model of career development for a multicultural workforce. *International Journal for the Advancement of Counseling, 15,* 187-195.

Coleman, V.D. & Barker, S.A. (1991). Barriers to the career development of multicultural populations. *Educational and Vocational Guidance, 52,* 25-29.

Coleman, VD. (2023). Dare to Care: Focus on Self-Care, 1st. In Weihman, M.R. *Dare to Care: Healthcare Superheroes Share Stories of Resilience, Hope & Inspiration.*

ISBN-13 979-8988427803.

Doran, G.T. *(1981). SMART Approach to Goal Setting.*

Fitts, W. (1964). *Tennessee Self-Concept Scale (TSCS).* Los Angeles, CA: Western Psychological Services.

Fitts, W. & Warren, W.L. (1996). *Tennessee Self-Concept Scale 2nd Edition (TSCS-2).* Los CA: Western Psychological Services.

Giles, A. & Ventura-Rozen, Galit. (2021). *Be Your Own Superhero.* In the Everyday Woman's

Guide to Doing What You Love. Heart Centered Women Publishing (HeartCenteredWomenPublishing.com)

Porter, H. (2018). *40/40 Rules: Wisdom from 40 Women over 40, Volume II.* Washington, Utah: Prosperity Publishing.

Super, D.E., Starishevsky, R., Matlin, N., & Jordaan, J.P. (1963). *Career development: Self-Concept theory. Essays in vocational development.* New York, New York: College Entrance Examination Board.

Learn more about Everyday Woman at www.everydaywoman.me

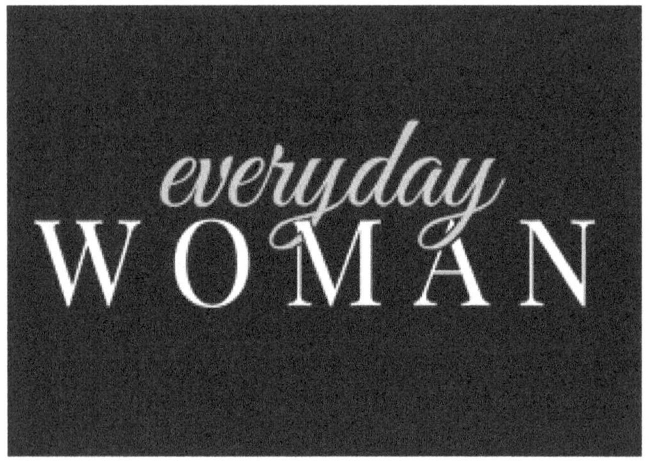

Learn more about becoming an author at www.sheempirecollective.com

Made in the USA
Columbia, SC
29 May 2025

58532015R00104